Mometrix
TEST PREPARATION

AP®

Music Theory Exam Secrets Study Guide

Dear Future Exam Success Story

First of all, **THANK YOU** for purchasing Mometrix study materials!

Second, congratulations! You are one of the few determined test-takers who are committed to doing whatever it takes to excel on your exam. **You have come to the right place.** We developed these study materials with one goal in mind: to deliver you the information you need in a format that's concise and easy to use.

In addition to optimizing your guide for the content of the test, we've outlined our recommended steps for breaking down the preparation process into small, attainable goals so you can make sure you stay on track.

We've also analyzed the entire test-taking process, identifying the most common pitfalls and showing how you can overcome them and be ready for any curveball the test throws you.

Standardized testing is one of the biggest obstacles on your road to success, which only increases the importance of doing well in the high-pressure, high-stakes environment of test day. Your results on this test could have a significant impact on your future, and this guide provides the information and practical advice to help you achieve your full potential on test day.

Your success is our success

We would love to hear from you! If you would like to share the story of your exam success or if you have any questions or comments in regard to our products, please contact us at **800-673-8175** or **support@mometrix.com**.

Thanks again for your business and we wish you continued success!

Sincerely,
The Mometrix Test Preparation Team

Need more help? Check out our flashcards at:
http://MometrixFlashcards.com/AP

Written and edited by the Mometrix Exam Secrets Test Prep Team
Printed in the United States of America

TABLE OF CONTENTS

Introduction

Thank you for purchasing this resource! You have made the choice to prepare yourself for a test that could have a huge impact on your future, and this guide is designed to help you be fully ready for test day. Obviously, it's important to have a solid understanding of the test material, but you also need to be prepared for the unique environment and stressors of the test, so that you can perform to the best of your abilities.

For this purpose, the first section that appears in this guide is the **Secret Keys**. We've devoted countless hours to meticulously researching what works and what doesn't, and we've boiled down our findings to the five most impactful steps you can take to improve your performance on the test. We start at the beginning with study planning and move through the preparation process, all the way to the testing strategies that will help you get the most out of what you know when you're finally sitting in front of the test.

We recommend that you start preparing for your test as far in advance as possible. However, if you've bought this guide as a last-minute study resource and only have a few days before your test, we recommend that you skip over the first two Secret Keys since they address a long-term study plan.

If you struggle with **test anxiety**, we strongly encourage you to check out our recommendations for how you can overcome it. Test anxiety is a formidable foe, but it can be beaten, and we want to make sure you have the tools you need to defeat it.

Secret Key #1 – Plan Big, Study Small

There's a lot riding on your performance. If you want to ace this test, you're going to need to keep your skills sharp and the material fresh in your mind. You need a plan that lets you review everything you need to know while still fitting in your schedule. We'll break this strategy down into three categories.

Information Organization

Start with the information you already have: the official test outline. From this, you can make a complete list of all the concepts you need to cover before the test. Organize these concepts into groups that can be studied together, and create a list of any related vocabulary you need to learn so you can brush up on any difficult terms. You'll want to keep this vocabulary list handy once you actually start studying since you may need to add to it along the way.

Time Management

Once you have your set of study concepts, decide how to spread them out over the time you have left before the test. Break your study plan into small, clear goals so you have a manageable task for each day and know exactly what you're doing. Then just focus on one small step at a time. When you manage your time this way, you don't need to spend hours at a time studying. Studying a small block of content for a short period each day helps you retain information better and avoid stressing over how much you have left to do. You can relax knowing that you have a plan to cover everything in time. In order for this strategy to be effective though, you have to start studying early and stick to your schedule. Avoid the exhaustion and futility that comes from last-minute cramming!

Study Environment

The environment you study in has a big impact on your learning. Studying in a coffee shop, while probably more enjoyable, is not likely to be as fruitful as studying in a quiet room. It's important to keep distractions to a minimum. You're only planning to study for a short block of time, so make the most of it. Don't pause to check your phone or get up to find a snack. It's also important to **avoid multitasking**. Research has consistently shown that multitasking will make your studying dramatically less effective. Your study area should also be comfortable and well-lit so you don't have the distraction of straining your eyes or sitting on an uncomfortable chair.

The time of day you study is also important. You want to be rested and alert. Don't wait until just before bedtime. Study when you'll be most likely to comprehend and remember. Even better, if you know what time of day your test will be, set that time aside for study. That way your brain will be used to working on that subject at that specific time and you'll have a better chance of recalling information.

Finally, it can be helpful to team up with others who are studying for the same test. Your actual studying should be done in as isolated an environment as possible, but the work of organizing the information and setting up the study plan can be divided up. In between study sessions, you can discuss with your teammates the concepts that you're all studying and quiz each other on the details. Just be sure that your teammates are as serious about the test as you are. If you find that your study time is being replaced with social time, you might need to find a new team.

Secret Key #2 – Make Your Studying Count

You're devoting a lot of time and effort to preparing for this test, so you want to be absolutely certain it will pay off. This means doing more than just reading the content and hoping you can remember it on test day. It's important to make every minute of study count. There are two main areas you can focus on to make your studying count.

Retention

It doesn't matter how much time you study if you can't remember the material. You need to make sure you are retaining the concepts. To check your retention of the information you're learning, try recalling it at later times with minimal prompting. Try carrying around flashcards and glance at one or two from time to time or ask a friend who's also studying for the test to quiz you.

To enhance your retention, look for ways to put the information into practice so that you can apply it rather than simply recalling it. If you're using the information in practical ways, it will be much easier to remember. Similarly, it helps to solidify a concept in your mind if you're not only reading it to yourself but also explaining it to someone else. Ask a friend to let you teach them about a concept you're a little shaky on (or speak aloud to an imaginary audience if necessary). As you try to summarize, define, give examples, and answer your friend's questions, you'll understand the concepts better and they will stay with you longer. Finally, step back for a big picture view and ask yourself how each piece of information fits with the whole subject. When you link the different concepts together and see them working together as a whole, it's easier to remember the individual components.

Finally, practice showing your work on any multi-step problems, even if you're just studying. Writing out each step you take to solve a problem will help solidify the process in your mind, and you'll be more likely to remember it during the test.

Modality

Modality simply refers to the means or method by which you study. Choosing a study modality that fits your own individual learning style is crucial. No two people learn best in exactly the same way, so it's important to know your strengths and use them to your advantage.

For example, if you learn best by visualization, focus on visualizing a concept in your mind and draw an image or a diagram. Try color-coding your notes, illustrating them, or creating symbols that will trigger your mind to recall a learned concept. If you learn best by hearing or discussing information, find a study partner who learns the same way or read aloud to yourself. Think about how to put the information in your own words. Imagine that you are giving a lecture on the topic and record yourself so you can listen to it later.

For any learning style, flashcards can be helpful. Organize the information so you can take advantage of spare moments to review. Underline key words or phrases. Use different colors for different categories. Mnemonic devices (such as creating a short list in which every item starts with the same letter) can also help with retention. Find what works best for you and use it to store the information in your mind most effectively and easily.

Secret Key #3 – Practice the Right Way

Your success on test day depends not only on how many hours you put into preparing, but also on whether you prepared the right way. It's good to check along the way to see if your studying is paying off. One of the most effective ways to do this is by taking practice tests to evaluate your progress. Practice tests are useful because they show exactly where you need to improve. Every time you take a practice test, pay special attention to these three groups of questions:

- The questions you got wrong
- The questions you had to guess on, even if you guessed right
- The questions you found difficult or slow to work through

This will show you exactly what your weak areas are, and where you need to devote more study time. Ask yourself why each of these questions gave you trouble. Was it because you didn't understand the material? Was it because you didn't remember the vocabulary? Do you need more repetitions on this type of question to build speed and confidence? Dig into those questions and figure out how you can strengthen your weak areas as you go back to review the material.

Additionally, many practice tests have a section explaining the answer choices. It can be tempting to read the explanation and think that you now have a good understanding of the concept. However, an explanation likely only covers part of the question's broader context. Even if the explanation makes perfect sense, **go back and investigate** every concept related to the question until you're positive you have a thorough understanding.

As you go along, keep in mind that the practice test is just that: practice. Memorizing these questions and answers will not be very helpful on the actual test because it is unlikely to have any of the same exact questions. If you only know the right answers to the sample questions, you won't be prepared for the real thing. **Study the concepts** until you understand them fully, and then you'll be able to answer any question that shows up on the test.

It's important to wait on the practice tests until you're ready. If you take a test on your first day of study, you may be overwhelmed by the amount of material covered and how much you need to learn. Work up to it gradually.

On test day, you'll need to be prepared for answering questions, managing your time, and using the test-taking strategies you've learned. It's a lot to balance, like a mental marathon that will have a big impact on your future. Like training for a marathon, you'll need to start slowly and work your way up. When test day arrives, you'll be ready.

Start with the strategies you've read in the first two Secret Keys—plan your course and study in the way that works best for you. If you have time, consider using multiple study resources to get different approaches to the same concepts. It can be helpful to see difficult concepts from more than one angle. Then find a good source for practice tests. Many times, the test website will suggest potential study resources or provide sample tests.

Practice Test Strategy

If you're able to find at least three practice tests, we recommend this strategy:

Untimed and Open-Book Practice

Take the first test with no time constraints and with your notes and study guide handy. Take your time and focus on applying the strategies you've learned.

Timed and Open-Book Practice

Take the second practice test open-book as well, but set a timer and practice pacing yourself to finish in time.

Timed and Closed-Book Practice

Take any other practice tests as if it were test day. Set a timer and put away your study materials. Sit at a table or desk in a quiet room, imagine yourself at the testing center, and answer questions as quickly and accurately as possible.

Keep repeating timed and closed-book tests on a regular basis until you run out of practice tests or it's time for the actual test. Your mind will be ready for the schedule and stress of test day, and you'll be able to focus on recalling the material you've learned.

Secret Key #4 – Pace Yourself

Once you're fully prepared for the material on the test, your biggest challenge on test day will be managing your time. Just knowing that the clock is ticking can make you panic even if you have plenty of time left. Work on pacing yourself so you can build confidence against the time constraints of the exam. Pacing is a difficult skill to master, especially in a high-pressure environment, so **practice is vital**.

Set time expectations for your pace based on how much time is available. For example, if a section has 60 questions and the time limit is 30 minutes, you know you have to average 30 seconds or less per question in order to answer them all. Although 30 seconds is the hard limit, set 25 seconds per question as your goal, so you reserve extra time to spend on harder questions. When you budget extra time for the harder questions, you no longer have any reason to stress when those questions take longer to answer.

Don't let this time expectation distract you from working through the test at a calm, steady pace, but keep it in mind so you don't spend too much time on any one question. Recognize that taking extra time on one question you don't understand may keep you from answering two that you do understand later in the test. If your time limit for a question is up and you're still not sure of the answer, mark it and move on, and come back to it later if the time and the test format allow. If the testing format doesn't allow you to return to earlier questions, just make an educated guess; then put it out of your mind and move on.

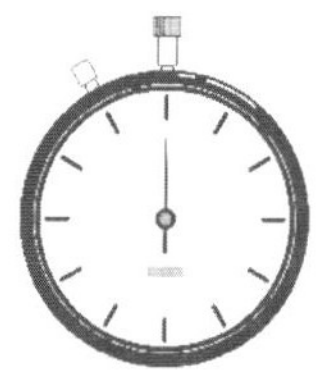

On the easier questions, be careful not to rush. It may seem wise to hurry through them so you have more time for the challenging ones, but it's not worth missing one if you know the concept and just didn't take the time to read the question fully. Work efficiently but make sure you understand the question and have looked at all of the answer choices, since more than one may seem right at first.

Even if you're paying attention to the time, you may find yourself a little behind at some point. You should speed up to get back on track, but do so wisely. Don't panic; just take a few seconds less on each question until you're caught up. Don't guess without thinking, but do look through the answer choices and eliminate any you know are wrong. If you can get down to two choices, it is often worthwhile to guess from those. Once you've chosen an answer, move on and don't dwell on any that you skipped or had to hurry through. If a question was taking too long, chances are it was one of the harder ones, so you weren't as likely to get it right anyway.

On the other hand, if you find yourself getting ahead of schedule, it may be beneficial to slow down a little. The more quickly you work, the more likely you are to make a careless mistake that will affect your score. You've budgeted time for each question, so don't be afraid to spend that time. Practice an efficient but careful pace to get the most out of the time you have.

Secret Key #5 – Have a Plan for Guessing

When you're taking the test, you may find yourself stuck on a question. Some of the answer choices seem better than others, but you don't see the one answer choice that is obviously correct. What do you do?

The scenario described above is very common, yet most test takers have not effectively prepared for it. Developing and practicing a plan for guessing may be one of the single most effective uses of your time as you get ready for the exam.

In developing your plan for guessing, there are three questions to address:

- When should you start the guessing process?
- How should you narrow down the choices?
- Which answer should you choose?

When to Start the Guessing Process

Unless your plan for guessing is to select C every time (which, despite its merits, is not what we recommend), you need to leave yourself enough time to apply your answer elimination strategies. Since you have a limited amount of time for each question, that means that if you're going to give yourself the best shot at guessing correctly, you have to decide quickly whether or not you will guess.

Of course, the best-case scenario is that you don't have to guess at all, so first, see if you can answer the question based on your knowledge of the subject and basic reasoning skills. Focus on the key words in the question and try to jog your memory of related topics. Give yourself a chance to bring the knowledge to mind, but once you realize that you don't have (or you can't access) the knowledge you need to answer the question, it's time to start the guessing process.

It's almost always better to start the guessing process too early than too late. It only takes a few seconds to remember something and answer the question from knowledge. Carefully eliminating wrong answer choices takes longer. Plus, going through the process of eliminating answer choices can actually help jog your memory.

Summary: Start the guessing process as soon as you decide that you can't answer the question based on your knowledge.

How to Narrow Down the Choices

The next chapter in this book (**Test-Taking Strategies**) includes a wide range of strategies for how to approach questions and how to look for answer choices to eliminate. You will definitely want to read those carefully, practice them, and figure out which ones work best for you. Here though, we're going to address a mindset rather than a particular strategy.

Your odds of guessing an answer correctly depend on how many options you are choosing from.

Number of options left	5	4	3	2	1
Odds of guessing correctly	20%	25%	33%	50%	100%

You can see from this chart just how valuable it is to be able to eliminate incorrect answers and make an educated guess, but there are two things that many test takers do that cause them to miss out on the benefits of guessing:

- Accidentally eliminating the correct answer
- Selecting an answer based on an impression

We'll look at the first one here, and the second one in the next section.

To avoid accidentally eliminating the correct answer, we recommend a thought exercise called **the $5 challenge**. In this challenge, you only eliminate an answer choice from contention if you are willing to bet $5 on it being wrong. Why $5? Five dollars is a small but not insignificant amount of money. It's an amount you could afford to lose but wouldn't want to throw away. And while losing $5 once might not hurt too much, doing it twenty times will set you back $100. In the same way, each small decision you make—eliminating a choice here, guessing on a question there—won't by itself impact your score very much, but when you put them all together, they can make a big difference. By holding each answer choice elimination decision to a higher standard, you can reduce the risk of accidentally eliminating the correct answer.

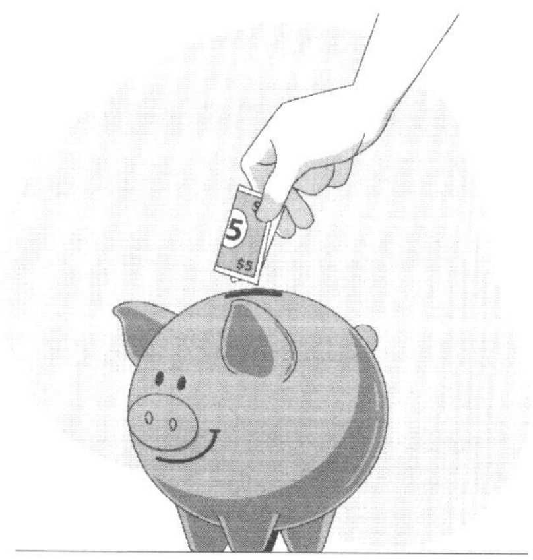

The $5 challenge can also be applied in a positive sense: If you are willing to bet $5 that an answer choice *is* correct, go ahead and mark it as correct.

Summary: Only eliminate an answer choice if you are willing to bet $5 that it is wrong.

Which Answer to Choose

You're taking the test. You've run into a hard question and decided you'll have to guess. You've eliminated all the answer choices you're willing to bet $5 on. Now you have to pick an answer. Why do we even need to talk about this? Why can't you just pick whichever one you feel like when the time comes?

The answer to these questions is that if you don't come into the test with a plan, you'll rely on your impression to select an answer choice, and if you do that, you risk falling into a trap. The test writers know that everyone who takes their test will be guessing on some of the questions, so they intentionally write wrong answer choices to seem plausible. You still have to pick an answer though, and if the wrong answer choices are designed to look right, how can you ever be sure that you're not falling for their trap? The best solution we've found to this dilemma is to take the decision out of your hands entirely. Here is the process we recommend:

Once you've eliminated any choices that you are confident (willing to bet $5) are wrong, select the first remaining choice as your answer.

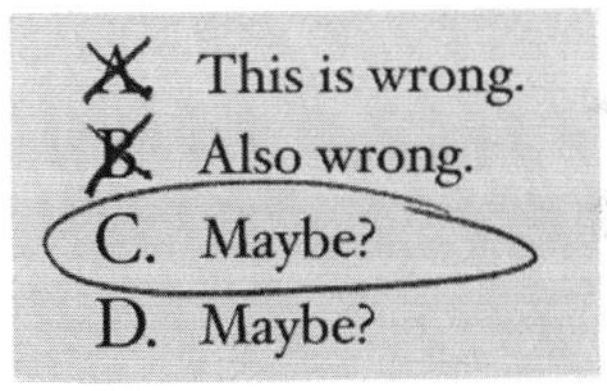

Whether you choose to select the first remaining choice, the second, or the last, the important thing is that you use some preselected standard. Using this approach guarantees that you will not be enticed into selecting an answer choice that looks right, because you are not basing your decision on how the answer choices look.

This is not meant to make you question your knowledge. Instead, it is to help you recognize the difference between your knowledge and your impressions. There's a huge difference between thinking an answer is right because of what you know, and thinking an answer is right because it looks or sounds like it should be right.

Summary: To ensure that your selection is appropriately random, make a predetermined selection from among all answer choices you have not eliminated.

Test-Taking Strategies

This section contains a list of test-taking strategies that you may find helpful as you work through the test. By taking what you know and applying logical thought, you can maximize your chances of answering any question correctly!

It is very important to realize that every question is different and every person is different: no single strategy will work on every question, and no single strategy will work for every person. That's why we've included all of them here, so you can try them out and determine which ones work best for different types of questions and which ones work best for you.

Question Strategies

READ CAREFULLY

Read the question and the answer choices carefully. Don't miss the question because you misread the terms. You have plenty of time to read each question thoroughly and make sure you understand what is being asked. Yet a happy medium must be attained, so don't waste too much time. You must read carefully and efficiently.

CONTEXTUAL CLUES

Look for contextual clues. If the question includes a word you are not familiar with, look at the immediate context for some indication of what the word might mean. Contextual clues can often give you all the information you need to decipher the meaning of an unfamiliar word. Even if you can't determine the meaning, you may be able to narrow down the possibilities enough to make a solid guess at the answer to the question.

PREFIXES

If you're having trouble with a word in the question or answer choices, try dissecting it. Take advantage of every clue that the word might include. Prefixes can be a huge help. Usually, they allow you to determine a basic meaning. *Pre-* means before, *post-* means after, *pro-* is positive, *de-* is negative. From prefixes, you can get an idea of the general meaning of the word and try to put it into context.

HEDGE WORDS

Watch out for critical hedge words, such as *likely, may, can, often, almost, mostly, usually, generally, rarely*, and *sometimes*. Question writers insert these hedge phrases to cover every possibility. Often an answer choice will be wrong simply because it leaves no room for exception. Be on guard for answer choices that have definitive words such as *exactly* and *always*.

SWITCHBACK WORDS

Stay alert for *switchbacks*. These are the words and phrases frequently used to alert you to shifts in thought. The most common switchback words are *but, although*, and *however*. Others include *nevertheless, on the other hand, even though, while, in spite of, despite*, and *regardless of*. Switchback words are important to catch because they can change the direction of the question or an answer choice.

⊘ FACE VALUE

When in doubt, use common sense. Accept the situation in the problem at face value. Don't read too much into it. These problems will not require you to make wild assumptions. If you have to go beyond creativity and warp time or space in order to have an answer choice fit the question, then you should move on and consider the other answer choices. These are normal problems rooted in reality. The applicable relationship or explanation may not be readily apparent, but it is there for you to figure out. Use your common sense to interpret anything that isn't clear.

Answer Choice Strategies

⊘ ANSWER SELECTION

The most thorough way to pick an answer choice is to identify and eliminate wrong answers until only one is left, then confirm it is the correct answer. Sometimes an answer choice may immediately seem right, but be careful. The test writers will usually put more than one reasonable answer choice on each question, so take a second to read all of them and make sure that the other choices are not equally obvious. As long as you have time left, it is better to read every answer choice than to pick the first one that looks right without checking the others.

⊘ ANSWER CHOICE FAMILIES

An answer choice family consists of two (in rare cases, three) answer choices that are very similar in construction and cannot all be true at the same time. If you see two answer choices that are direct opposites or parallels, one of them is usually the correct answer. For instance, if one answer choice says that quantity *x* increases and another either says that quantity *x* decreases (opposite) or says that quantity *y* increases (parallel), then those answer choices would fall into the same family. An answer choice that doesn't match the construction of the answer choice family is more likely to be incorrect. Most questions will not have answer choice families, but when they do appear, you should be prepared to recognize them.

⊘ ELIMINATE ANSWERS

Eliminate answer choices as soon as you realize they are wrong, but make sure you consider all possibilities. If you are eliminating answer choices and realize that the last one you are left with is also wrong, don't panic. Start over and consider each choice again. There may be something you missed the first time that you will realize on the second pass.

⊘ AVOID FACT TRAPS

Don't be distracted by an answer choice that is factually true but doesn't answer the question. You are looking for the choice that answers the question. Stay focused on what the question is asking for so you don't accidentally pick an answer that is true but incorrect. Always go back to the question and make sure the answer choice you've selected actually answers the question and is not merely a true statement.

⊘ EXTREME STATEMENTS

In general, you should avoid answers that put forth extreme actions as standard practice or proclaim controversial ideas as established fact. An answer choice that states the "process should be used in certain situations, if..." is much more likely to be correct than one that states the "process should be discontinued completely." The first is a calm rational statement and doesn't even make a definitive, uncompromising stance, using a hedge word *if* to provide wiggle room, whereas the second choice is far more extreme.

☑ Benchmark

As you read through the answer choices and you come across one that seems to answer the question well, mentally select that answer choice. This is not your final answer, but it's the one that will help you evaluate the other answer choices. The one that you selected is your benchmark or standard for judging each of the other answer choices. Every other answer choice must be compared to your benchmark. That choice is correct until proven otherwise by another answer choice beating it. If you find a better answer, then that one becomes your new benchmark. Once you've decided that no other choice answers the question as well as your benchmark, you have your final answer.

☑ Predict the Answer

Before you even start looking at the answer choices, it is often best to try to predict the answer. When you come up with the answer on your own, it is easier to avoid distractions and traps because you will know exactly what to look for. The right answer choice is unlikely to be word-for-word what you came up with, but it should be a close match. Even if you are confident that you have the right answer, you should still take the time to read each option before moving on.

General Strategies

☑ Tough Questions

If you are stumped on a problem or it appears too hard or too difficult, don't waste time. Move on! Remember though, if you can quickly check for obviously incorrect answer choices, your chances of guessing correctly are greatly improved. Before you completely give up, at least try to knock out a couple of possible answers. Eliminate what you can and then guess at the remaining answer choices before moving on.

☑ Check Your Work

Since you will probably not know every term listed and the answer to every question, it is important that you get credit for the ones that you do know. Don't miss any questions through careless mistakes. If at all possible, try to take a second to look back over your answer selection and make sure you've selected the correct answer choice and haven't made a costly careless mistake (such as marking an answer choice that you didn't mean to mark). This quick double check should more than pay for itself in caught mistakes for the time it costs.

☑ Pace Yourself

It's easy to be overwhelmed when you're looking at a page full of questions; your mind is confused and full of random thoughts, and the clock is ticking down faster than you would like. Calm down and maintain the pace that you have set for yourself. Especially as you get down to the last few minutes of the test, don't let the small numbers on the clock make you panic. As long as you are on track by monitoring your pace, you are guaranteed to have time for each question.

☑ Don't Rush

It is very easy to make errors when you are in a hurry. Maintaining a fast pace in answering questions is pointless if it makes you miss questions that you would have gotten right otherwise. Test writers like to include distracting information and wrong answers that seem right. Taking a little extra time to avoid careless mistakes can make all the difference in your test score. Find a pace that allows you to be confident in the answers that you select.

✅ KEEP MOVING

Panicking will not help you pass the test, so do your best to stay calm and keep moving. Taking deep breaths and going through the answer elimination steps you practiced can help to break through a stress barrier and keep your pace.

Final Notes

The combination of a solid foundation of content knowledge and the confidence that comes from practicing your plan for applying that knowledge is the key to maximizing your performance on test day. As your foundation of content knowledge is built up and strengthened, you'll find that the strategies included in this chapter become more and more effective in helping you quickly sift through the distractions and traps of the test to isolate the correct answer.

Now that you're preparing to move forward into the test content chapters of this book, be sure to keep your goal in mind. As you read, think about how you will be able to apply this information on the test. If you've already seen sample questions for the test and you have an idea of the question format and style, try to come up with questions of your own that you can answer based on what you're reading. This will give you valuable practice applying your knowledge in the same ways you can expect to on test day.

Good luck and good studying!

Musical Terminology

Interval

An interval is described as the distance between any two notes. It is a tool as well as a foundational component of musical notation for symbolizing the distance between any two pitches. Intervals are identified numerically as the number of pitches in between and including the two notes in discussion. To find an interval in musical notation, count all the lines and spaces in between the two notes, and add the two notes that make the interval. Intervals are labeled by ordinal numbers, for example, second, third, fourth, and so on. The intervals of a first and an eighth both have special names: prime or unison for a first and octave for an eighth. If the top note of an interval is contained within the major key of the bottom note, the interval will be either major or perfect depending on its size; seconds, third, sixths and sevenths are major intervals while fourths, fifths, and octaves are perfect. Other interval qualities are minor, augmented, and diminished.

Major and Perfect Intervals

Major and perfect both describe intervals in which the top note is contained within the major scale of the bottom note. If the top note of an interval is contained within the major key of the bottom note, the interval will be either major or perfect depending on its size; seconds, third, sixths and sevenths are major intervals, whereas fourths, fifths, and octaves are perfect. For example, to find the interval from G up to F#, count the scale degrees of the G major scale—G, A, B, C, D, E, and F#. Because F# is in the key of G major, it is a major seventh interval. The interval from C up to F would then be a perfect fourth interval because F is in the key of C major. An interval cannot be both major and perfect, but must be one or the other. Perfect intervals can only be altered to become diminished and augmented, whereas major intervals can be altered to become both diminished and augmented as well as minor intervals.

Harmonic and Melodic Intervals

An interval is described as the distance between any two notes. As such, two musical notes can be played simultaneously as well as in succession to each other. Intervals in which the two notes are played at the same time are considered harmonic intervals, similarly to the concept of harmony, in which the root comes from the Greek word that means *joined*. Harmonic intervals sound at the same time, and in notation, the two notes appear to be stacked one on top of the other. Melodic intervals, on the other hand, describe an interval in which the two notes are played in succession, similarly to the concept of melody, in which a series of pitches can be sung in a single line of music. Melodic intervals sound as one pitch followed by the other, whereas in notation, they appear one after the other. Although the pitches of harmonic and melodic intervals differ in relative position to each other, the distance between the two notes is measured independently of their relative positions.

Augmentation and Diminution of Intervals

Intervals as identified by both their size and by their quality, for example, perfect fourth, minor second, and so on. The size of an interval refers to the distance between the two pitches, and the quality of an interval refers to whether it is perfect, major, minor, augmented, or diminished. Certain intervals can be made larger or smaller through augmentation or diminution. Generally, augmenting an interval makes it larger by a half step; diminishing an interval makes it smaller by a half step. Specifically, an augmented interval, for example, an augmented fifth, is an interval that is a half step larger than either a perfect or major interval. Similarly, a diminished interval, for example, a diminished second, is an interval that is a half step smaller than either a minor or perfect interval.

For major intervals, the order of possible qualities from smallest to largest, each separated by a half step is diminished, minor, major, and augmented. For perfect intervals, the order of possible qualities from smallest to largest, each separated by a half step is diminished, perfect, and augmented.

Determining Intervals

When determining the quality and size of an interval, there are several considerations to keep in mind. perfect intervals are the fourth, fifth, and octave; major intervals are the second, third, sixth, and seventh. When a perfect interval is lowered or raised by a half step, it becomes either a diminished interval or augmented interval, respectively. Major intervals first become minor intervals when lowered by a half step and then diminished upon another lowering of a half step. Consider the bottom note as tonic to determine major and minor intervals; if the notes are within the major scale, the interval must be a major or perfect interval. In the first example, the B is the diatonic fourth scale degree in the F# major scale, so it is an interval of a perfect fourth. In the second example, the F# is the diatonic third scale degree in the D major scale, so it is an interval of a major third. In the third example, the Ab is not the diatonic fifth scale degree in the D major scale, but is a half step below the fifth scale degree, so it is an interval of a diminished fifth.

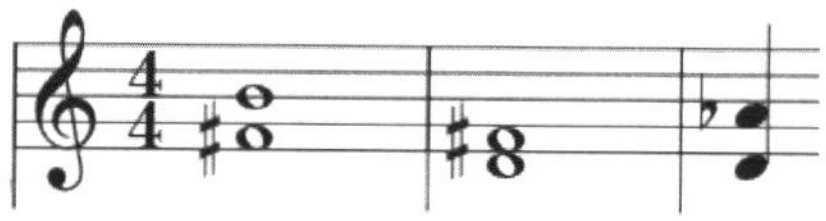

Compound Intervals

Compound intervals are intervals that are larger than an octave. To find the size of a compound interval in musical notation, count all the lines and spaces in between the two notes, and add the two notes that make the interval. Intervals are labeled by ordinal numbers, so compound intervals would also be labeled as ninth, tenth, eleventh, and so on. The quality of a compound interval is the same as its corresponding interval that is less than an octave. For example, the interval of D to B within an octave is a major sixth. The compound interval of D to B, which is a thirteenth, would also be a major thirteenth. For another way to find the quality of the compound interval, subtract seven from the number of the compound interval to assess the corresponding interval that is less than one octave. (The corresponding interval to a fifteenth would be 15 – 7 = 8: the octave.)

Inverted Intervals

Inverted intervals occur when the pitches of a certain interval are switched so that the lower note becomes the higher note and the higher note becomes the lower note. For example, the interval of a major third from C up to E becomes an inverted interval of a minor sixth from E up to C. In relation to the sizes of intervals and their inverted forms, the number of an interval and its inverted form always add up to nine, except for the octave, which stays an octave when inverted. Therefore, seconds always become sevenths, thirds become sixths, fourths become fifths, fifths become fourths, sixths become thirds, and sevenths become seconds. In relation to the quality of an interval and its inverted form, major intervals become minor intervals, augmented intervals become diminished intervals, minor intervals become major intervals, and diminished intervals become augmented intervals. Perfect intervals always stay perfect when inverted.

Major Triad

A major triad consists of three pitches: the first, third, and fifth scale degrees of a major scale. The first scale degree acts as the tonic or root of the chord. The distance between the root and the third of the major triad is always four half steps; this is one distinguishing marker between major and minor triads (minor triads only have three half steps between the root and the third of the chord). The distance between the root and the fifth of the chord is always a perfect fifth. Without these exact distances, the triad is not a major chord. When inverted, the triad maintains the same quality. For example, the root position of a C major triad consists of C – E – G; the first inversion consists of E – G – C; the second inversion consists of G – C – E. All of these are in the C major harmony.

Changing a Major Triad to an Augmented Triad

When changing a major triad to an augmented triad, only the fifth note of the chord is changed. The root and the third of the chord stay the same, whereas the fifth note of the chord is raised by a half step. For example, to change C major triad, C – E – G to C augmented triad, the fifth note of the chord, G in this case, is raised by a half step so that the augmented triad spells C – E – G#. The distance between the root and the third of an augmented chord is four half steps, whereas the distance between the root and the fifth note of an augmented chord is an interval of an augmented fifth. Care must be taken to ensure that the name of the altered pitch contains the same letter name to reflect that the pitch has been altered; for example, the fifth note of the previous example cannot be called Ab but must be called G# to reflect the alteration.

Changing a Major Triad into a Diminished Triad

When changing a major triad to a diminished triad, there are two steps that must be taken: the third and the fifth must be lowered by a half step. For example, to change C major triad, C – E – G, to C diminished triad, the third and fifth notes of the chord, E and G in this case, are both lowered by a half step so that the diminished triad spells C – Eb – Gb. The distance between the root and the third of a diminished triad is three half steps, whereas the interval between the root and the fifth of the diminished triad is a diminished fifth. Care must be taken to ensure that the names of the altered pitches contain the same letter name to reflect that the pitch has been altered; for example, the fifth note of the previous example cannot be called F but must be called Gb to reflect the alteration.

Determining the Root and Quality of a Triad Within an Excerpt

When determining the root and quality of a triad harmony within an excerpt, one must take care to make a note of all the pitches present. First, assemble all the pitches present; when a pitch is doubled, it is not necessary to note it twice. If done carefully, there should be three prominent pitches from which to determine the root and quality. Once the pitches are assembled, the next step is to order them and stack them by thirds. This step may take some trial and error, but once the pitches are stacked by thirds, then the root and quality of the chord can be more easily determined. The bottom pitch of the stacked triad is the root. To determine the quality of the triad, count the half steps between the root and the third. If there are three half steps, the chord is either minor or diminished; if there are four half steps, the chord is major, perfect, or augmented. Next, determine the interval between the root and the fifth of the chord. If the interval between the root and fifth is a diminished fifth, then the chord is a diminished triad. If the interval between the root and the fifth is a perfect fifth, then one of two possibilities exist: three half steps between the root and the third plus a perfect fifth means a minor triad; four half steps between the root and the third plus a perfect fifth means a major triad or a perfect triad depending on context.

Figured Bass

Figured bass stems from the common practice during the Baroque era in which composers wrote a bass line with symbols for what specific harmonies were to be played; the exact notes to be played for the keyboard or continuo were not provided. Musicians at the time were adept at realizing the figured bass and improvising music based solely on a bass line and corresponding harmonies. The chords were represented by Roman numerals for their respective scale degree and function within the music. For example, the Roman numeral V would represent the dominant chord of G major as the root note of G major is the fifth note in the C major harmony. Further symbols indicate whether a triad is in its root position or in inversion: the symbol 5/3 indicates root position; 6/3 indicates first inversion; and 6/4 indicates second inversion.

Dominate Seventh Chord

The dominant seventh chord describes the V7 chord within functional harmony. The root of the chord is the fifth scale degree within the scale and typically leads to I, or the tonic. The third and fifth of the seventh chord are the same as in a major triad: four half steps between the root and the third and an interval of a perfect fifth from the root to the fifth. The fourth additional note above the root has an interval of a minor seventh between the root and the fourth note. All four notes of the seventh chord are spaced a third apart so that when written on the staff, they are, in root position, either all lines or all spaces. The name of the chord describes the dominant function of the chord (V) and the interval of a seventh within the chord.

Major Seventh Chord

The major seventh chord contains a major triad between the first three notes and the interval of a major seventh between the first and fourth notes. The third and fifth of the seventh chord are the same as in a major triad: four half steps between the root and the third and an interval of a perfect fifth from the root to the fifth. The fourth additional note above the root has an interval of a major seventh between the root and the fourth note. All four notes of the seventh chord are spaced a third apart so that when written on the staff, they are, in root position, either all lines or all spaces. The name of the chord describes the quality of both the triad and the interval within the chord.

Minor Seventh Chord

The minor seventh chord contains a minor triad between the first three notes and the interval of a minor seventh between the first and fourth notes. The third and fifth of the seventh chord are the same as in a minor triad: three half steps between the root and the third and an interval of a perfect fifth from the root to the fifth. The fourth additional note above the root has an interval of a minor seventh between the root and the fourth note. All four notes of the seventh chord are spaced a third apart so that when written on the staff, they are, in root position, either all lines or all spaces. The name of the chord describes the quality of both the triad and the interval within the chord.

Half-Diminished Seventh Chord

The half-diminished seventh chord contains a diminished triad between the first three notes and the interval of a minor seventh between the first and fourth notes. The third and fifth of the seventh chord are the same as in a diminished triad: three half steps between the root and the third and an interval of a diminished fifth from the root to the fifth. The fourth additional note above the root has an interval of a minor seventh between the root and the fourth note. All four notes of the seventh chord are spaced a third apart so that when written on the staff, they are, in root position, either all lines or all spaces. The name of the chord describes the quality of both the triad and the interval within the chord.

Fully Diminished Seventh Chord

The fully diminished seventh chord contains a diminished triad between the first three notes and the interval of a diminished seventh between the first and fourth notes. The third and fifth of the seventh chord are the same as in a diminished triad: three half steps between the root and the third and an interval of a diminished fifth from the root to the fifth. The fourth additional note above the root has an interval of a diminished seventh between the root and the fourth note. All four notes of the seventh chord are spaced a third apart so that when written on the staff, they are, in root position, either all lines or all spaces. The name of the chord describes the quality of both the triad and the intervals within the chord, all of which are diminished.

Figured Bass Symbols for Seventh Chords

The figured bass symbols for seventh chords and their inversions describe the relationship between the root and the seventh of the chord, indicating the distance from the bottom note to those pitches. In root position, the distance between the bottom note and the root is unison, whereas the distance between the bottom note and the seventh is seven; the unison is redundant to reiterate, and so the figured bass for a seventh in root position is merely seven. In first inversion, the distance between the bottom note and the seventh is an interval of a fifth, whereas the distance between the bottom note and the root is an interval of a sixth, so the figured bass is 6/5. In second inversion, the distance between the bottom note and the seventh is a third, whereas the distance between the bottom note and the root is a fourth, so the figured bass is 4/3. In third inversion, the distance between the bottom note and the seventh is unison, and the distance between the bottom note and the root is a second, so the figured bass is two.

Diatonic Scales

Diatonic scales have seven distinct pitches spanning an octave in a specific ordering of whole and half steps. The scales that are considered to be diatonic include the major scale and all minor scales. For the major scale, the order of whole and half steps are as follows: tonic - whole step - whole step - half step - whole step - whole step - whole step - half step. The pitches are ordered in this way so that the half steps are as far away from each other as possible. The minor scales are altered diatonic scales, but each still have seven distinct pitches in specific ordering. For the natural scale, the order of whole and half steps are as follows: tonic - whole step - half step - whole step - whole step - half step - whole step - whole step. For the harmonic scale, the order of whole and half steps are as follows: tonic - whole step - half step - whole step - whole step - half step - whole plus half step - whole step. For the ascending melodic scale, the order of whole and half steps are as follows: tonic - whole step - half step - whole step - whole step - whole step - whole step - half step; the descending pattern follows the natural scale pattern.

Major Scale

The major scale is a diatonic scale in which there are seven pitches within an octave. The pitches are organized by whole and half steps so that the pattern for major scales is as follows: tonic - whole step - whole step - half step - whole step - whole step - whole step - half step. The scale contains the exact same sharps or flats from its relative key signature. For example, for the scale of C major there are zero flats. Therefore, the pitches of the scale starting with the tonic note, C, are as follows: C - D - E - F - G - A - B - C. The major scale is made up of two tetrachords—C - D - E - F—and the tetrachord—G - A - B - C. Each tetrachord contains the starting note then whole step - whole step - half step.

Tetrachords Within a Major Scale

Tetrachords are the basic building blocks of a major scale. Each major scale is made up of two tetrachords. A tetrachord is structured so that the starting note is followed by a whole step, a whole step, and a half step. For example, a tetrachord starting on D would be as follows: D - E - F# - G. To make a major scale, a tetrachord could be added in front of or behind the D tetrachord. If added in front, the scale would be G - A - B - C plus D - E - F# - G to make the G major scale. If added behind, then the scale would be D - E - F# - G plus A - B - C# - D to make the D major scale. Without the structure of the two tetrachords, the major scale would not have the same order of whole and half sharps necessary to make it the diatonic scale that it is.

Natural, Harmonic, and Melodic Minor Scales

The natural, harmonic, and melodic minor scales all have the same minor key signature; however, certain alterations create the harmonic and melodic minor scales. The minor scale follows the exact same key signature as the major key signature that it is related to, usually three half steps above the minor key. For example, the relative major key of E minor would be three half steps or G major scale. A G major scale has one sharp in it—F#—so E minor also has the one same sharp. The natural minor contains just the sharps or flats of the key signature. The harmonic minor alters the seventh note so that it is raised by a half step. The melodic minor alters the sixth and seventh notes ascending so that they are raised by half steps but cancels the alterations on the descending melodic minor scale.

Chromatic Scale

The chromatic scale describes a scale in which all the pitches are separated by half steps. For the chromatic scale starting on C, the pitches would be C – C# – D – D# – E – F – F# – G – G# – A – A# – B – C to make thirteen notes of the chromatic scale. When notating the chromatic scale, it is helpful to write sharps for the ascending scale and flats for the descending scale so as not to confuse the pitch names with each other. The chromatic scale covers every note going up or going down in the modern tuning of Western instruments.

Whole Tone Scale

The whole tone scale describes a scale in which all pitches are separated by whole steps. There are only two whole tone scales; for the whole tone scale starting on C, the pitches would be C – D – E – F# – G# – A# – C to make six tones of the whole tone scale. For the whole tone scale starting on B, the pitches would be B – C# – D# – F – G – A – B. The pitches are written in such a way that one letter name will always be skipped. The pitches in a whole tone scale are equally spaced, so there are no tendency tones as in the leading tone or suspension voice leading in a diatonic scale. In both whole tone scales, there is a sense of vagueness because there is no clear tonic movement.

Pentatonic Scale

The pentatonic scale describes a scale in which there are only five pitches. The most common pentatonic scale in Western music is the one found on the black keys of the piano: C# – D# – F# – G# – A#. The pattern of whole and half steps is as follows: starting note – whole step – whole plus half step – whole step – whole step. This scale can be thought of as a diatonic scale with two missing pitches. There are two types of pentatonic scales: hemitonic and anhemitonic. Hemitonic pentatonic scales have at least one semitone or half step within the scale. Anhemitonic pentatonic scales do not have any semitones within the scale, such as the pentatonic scale in the example.

Dorian Mode

The Dorian mode can be most easily described as the scale that occurs on the white notes of a keyboard from D to D. The pattern of whole and half steps that occurs in Dorian mode is as follows: starting pitch – whole step – half step – whole step – whole step – whole step – half step – whole step. The half steps occur between scale degrees two and three and scale degrees six and seven. When tasked with writing Dorian mode, one can think of the major scale – D major scale in this example – and simply lower the fourth and seventh pitches by a half step so that F# becomes F, and C# becomes C.

Ionian Mode

The Ionian mode can be most easily described as the scale that occurs on the white notes of a keyboard from C to C. The pattern of whole and half steps that occurs in Ionian mode is as follows:

starting pitch - whole step - whole step - half step - whole step - whole step - whole step - half step. The half steps occur between scale degrees three and four, and between seven and eight. When writing the Ionian mode, one can think of the major scale as it is the same as the Ionian mode.

Phrygian Mode

The Phrygian mode can be more easily described as the scale that occurs on the white notes of a keyboard from E to E. The pattern of whole and half steps that occurs in Phrygian mode is as follows: starting note - half step - whole step - whole step - whole step - half step - whole step - whole step. The half steps occur between scale degrees one and two and between scale degrees five and six. When tasked with writing Phrygian mode, one can think of the natural minor scale—E natural minor in this example—and simply lower the second note by a half step so that F# becomes F natural.

Lydian Mode

The Lydian mode can be most easily described as the scale that occurs on the white notes of a keyboard from F to F. The pattern of whole and half steps that occurs in Lydian mode is as follows: starting pitch - whole step - whole step - whole step - half step - whole step - whole step - half step. The half steps occur between scale degrees four and five and between scale degrees seven and eight. When tasked with writing the Lydian mode, one can think of the major scale—F major scale in this example—and simply raise the fourth pitch by a half step so that Bb becomes B natural.

Mixolydian Mode

The Mixolydian mode can be most easily described as the scale that occurs on the white notes of a keyboard from G to G. The pattern of whole and half steps that occurs in the Mixolydian mode is as follows: starting pitch - whole step - whole step - half step - whole step - whole step - half step - whole step. The half steps occur between scale degrees three and four and between scale degrees six and seven. When tasked with writing the Mixolydian mode, one can think of the major scale—G major scale in this example—and simply lower the seventh pitch by a half step so that F# becomes F natural.

Aeolian Mode

The Aeolian mode can be most easily described as the scale that occurs on the white notes of a keyboard from A to A. The pattern of whole and half steps that occurs in Aeolian mode is as follows: starting pitch - whole step - half step - whole step - whole step - half step - whole step - whole step. The half steps occur between scale degrees two and three and between scale degrees five and six. When tasked with writing the Aeolian mode, one can think of the natural minor scale—A natural minor scale in this example—because it is the same scale.

Locrian Mode

The Locrian mode can be most easily described as the scale that occurs on the white notes of a keyboard from B to B. The pattern of whole and half steps that occurs in Locrian mode is as follows: starting pitch - half step - whole step - whole step - half step - whole step - whole step - whole step. The half steps occur between scale degrees one and two and between scale degrees four and five. When tasked with writing the Locrian mode, one can think of the natural minor scale—B natural minor scale in this example—and simply lower the second and fifth pitches by a half step so that C# becomes C natural and F# becomes F natural.

Steps Needed to Determine the Name of a Given Mode

One of the best approaches to determining the name of a given mode is based on the fact that each mode is associated with a white key mode on the keyboard. For example, the Locrian mode occurs on the white notes of a keyboard from B to B or the seventh scale degree of the C major scale. First, find the major key signature corresponding to the mode by looking at all the accidentals in the mode. Once the major key has been found, the first note of the mode then corresponds to the scale degree in that major key. For example, in the mode F – G – Ab – Bb – C – D – Eb – F, the corresponding key signature is that of Eb major: Bb, Eb, and Ab. In the key of Eb major, F is the second scale degree, so the mode must be the F Dorian mode.

Grand Staff

The parts of grand staff that are related to rhythm include the time signature, the bar lines, and the measures. The time signature indicates two things: the top number describes the number of beats within each measure, and the bottom number describes the note value that receives each beat. For example, for the time signature 2/4, there are two beats in each measure, and the quarter note receives the beat. The next component of a grand staff that is related to rhythm is the bar line. Each bar line delineates each measure within the piece. The measure then, helps to keep a metrical beat within the piece so that there is always a downbeat to the rhythm.

Simple Meter and Compound Meter

Both simple meter and compound meter describe the ordering of beats within a measure. However, simple meter features the most basic beat per measure. Examples include 2/4, 2/2, 3/4/ 3/2, 4/4, and 4/2. Compound meters describe meters that still feature two, three, or four basic beats but can be subdivided into smaller counts. Time signatures that have six, nine, or twelve are examples of compound meters. For example, in the time signature 6/8, there are two basic duple beats, but each of the beats can be subdivided into three eighth notes. Compound meters can always be divided by the number three, whereas simple meters cannot.

Dot Following a Note Versus a Double Dot Following the Note

When a dot follows a note, it indicates that half of the note value should be added to the overall count. For example, in a common time piece, a dotted quarter note will be held for one quarter beat plus an eighth beat (half of a quarter note) or one and a half beats. A dotted whole note would be held for a total of six beats: four from the whole note and two from half of its value. A double dot indicates that three quarters of the note value should be added to the overall count. For example, a doubly dotted quarter note would be held for one quarter beat plus an eighth beat plus a sixteenth beat. A doubly dotted whole note would be held for a total of seven beats: four from the whole note plus three more beats from the double dot (three quarters of a whole note).

Anacrusis

An anacrusis occurs when there is a pickup or upbeat to the beginning of a piece; it creates an incomplete measure less than the required beats per measure. Usually the last measure of the entire piece will contain the rest of the beats. For example, in a piece of music that has a common time signature, there is at the beginning of the piece an incomplete measure of just the fourth beat. This is the anacrusis. The final measure of the piece is also incomplete and contains beats one through three. These two measures together make up the required four beats per measure that the time signature indicates.

Metric Accent and an Agogic Accent

Both metric and agogic accents are rhythmic; that is, the tones that are accented are not louder dynamically than the surrounding notes but rhythmically emphasized instead. An agogic accent describes a rhythmic accent that occurs when a note is sustained longer than the surrounding notes on a beat that is usually considered a weak beat. In common time, the weak beats are two and four. For example, a half note that occurs on the second beat of a measure would be considered an agogic accent. A metric accent occurs naturally on the downbeat, which is considered to be the strongest beat of each measure in all time signatures. In common time, the strongest beat is the downbeat, followed by the third beat; beats two and four are considered weak beats. In 3/4, the downbeat is considered to be the strong beat, whereas beats two and three are weaker.

Augmentation and Diminution of Rhythm

Augmentation and diminution of rhythm refers to the temporal changes of a repeated melody. Rhythmic augmentation takes place when a certain melody is repeated with longer note values. Oftentimes, the rhythmic values are double the rhythmic values of the original melody. For example, a certain melody uses eighth notes the first time; when it is repeated, it uses quarter notes instead. Rhythmic diminution takes place when the pitches of a certain melody are repeated with shorter note values. Oftentimes, the rhythmic values are half of the original rhythmic values. For example, a certain melody uses quarter notes; when it is repeated, the altered melody uses eighth notes instead.

Syncopation and Hemiola

Both syncopation and hemiola act as changes of the regular rhythm in a deliberate manner. Syncopation can occur when accented notes are placed on normally weak beats: in 4/4, beats two and four, and in 3/4, beats two or three. It can also occur through agogic accents, when a longer note on a weak beat creates a rhythmic accent. Dynamic accents on weak beats also create a syncopated rhythm as well as the use of rests on strong beats. Hemiola occurs when the pulsing rhythm changes from pulses of two to three or pulses of three to two. For example, in a 6/8 time signature, a pulsing pattern of six eighth notes changes to three quarter notes in which the grouped pattern becomes two eighth notes instead of three.

Motive and Theme

Motive and theme both relate to similar melodic devices in which a musical idea is used throughout a piece of music as a recognizable aspect of the music and its development. However, many differences exist to distinguish a motive from a theme. A motive tends to be a short melodic or rhythmic idea that is repeated throughout a piece of music. When a motive appears throughout a piece of music, it serves as a unifying aspect of the music. A theme tends to be a longer musical idea, usually several measures, and can contain a recurring motive. Themes are the basic building blocks of thematic transformation in which a theme is developed by changing it in different ways.

Motivic Transformation

Motivic transformation refers to the change of the melodic idea that can occur over the development of a musical work. Common musical devices used in motivic transformation include repetition, sequence, imitation, fragmentation, augmentation, and diminution. Repetition takes place when the motive is repeated in exactly the same way. Sequence occurs when a motive is repeated on a different starting pitch but with all the same exact intervallic relationships. Imitation occurs when a motive is repeated in another voice, such as the tenor voice instead of the soprano voice. Fragmentation occurs when only a part of the motive appears. Augmentation occurs when the rhythmic values within the motive are doubled. Conversely, diminution occurs when the rhythmic values within the motive are halved. The motivic transformation tools of retrograde and inversion both refer to a manipulation of the sequence of pitches within a certain melody. Retrograde refers to a melody that has its pitches written backwards so that the ending pitch becomes the beginning pitch. For example, a melody C-D-G-G-E-F-A becomes, through retrograde, A-F-E-G-G-D-C. Inversion, or melodic inversion, refers to a melody that has the direction of the pitches, whether ascending or descending, switched. For example, a melody that starts on C goes up an interval of a fifth, down a second, up a third, and then up a fourth becomes, through inversion, a melody that starts on C, goes down an interval of a fifth, up a second, down a third, and then down a fourth.

Conjunct and Disjunct Melody

The terms *conjunct* and *disjunct* refer to the movement of the pitches within a certain melody. A conjunct melody moves primarily by steps rather than by leaps, whereas a disjunct melody moves primarily by leaps rather than by steps. An example of a conjunct melody is the folk tune "London Bridge Is Falling Down." The pitches in the beginning of the tune move up to a neighbor note and then down in a stepwise manner. An example of a disjunct melody is beginning part of the tune "Twinkle, Twinkle, Little Star." The pitches in the first phrase jump up an interval of a fifth before continuing on as a conjunct melody.

Countermelody

A countermelody is considered to be a functioning secondary melody that is usually played simultaneously with the primary melody but can also follow the main melody or occur part way through the theme. It generally follows a different rhythm and contour from the primary melody so that it is distinct as a separate melodic entity. The countermelody serves as a point of interest in a musical texture that has a basic melody and accompaniment, adding to the complexity and richness of the music. It can add variation to a repeated melody line without changing the primary features of the main melody. The countermelody differs from an accompaniment in that it has a melodic character of its own.

Chords with Dominant Functions

In functional harmony, chords with dominant function refer to chords that most strongly tend to resolve to the tonic or chords with tonic function. Chords with dominant function usually create tension and instability that lead to resolution with the tonic. The seventh and fourth scale degree in any key naturally creates this tension that wants to lead by a half step up to the tonic note or down by a half step to the third scale degree, respectively. Therefore, chords with the seventh scale degree in them are chords with dominant function. These include the dominant V chord, the dominant V7, and the leading chord vii°. All of these chords contain the seventh scale degree of the key, with the V7 and vii° containing an added tritone relationship that creates further instability.

Chords with Predominant Function

In functional harmony, chords with predominant function refer to chords that tend to create a sense of movement away from the tonic while also preparing for dominant chords. Chords with predominant function usually include the first and fourth scale degrees that prepare for movement to dominant chords. The tonic note within chords with predominant functions descends to the leading tone in a dominant chord. These scale degrees are also considered to be far in distance from the dominant of dominant chords. Chords with predominant function include the subdominant IV, the supertonic ii, and the submediant vi, all of which contain either the fourth scale degree, the first scale degree, or both.

Tonic Chord

In functional harmony, the tonic chord refers to the I chord, which is the strongest and most stable functioning chord. The tonic chord defines the key of a piece and is usually present in both the beginning and ending of a musical work. The tonic chord is made up of the first, third, and fifth scale degrees of the key, all of which make up the most stable pitches in functional harmony. Many of the other scale degrees become tendency tones toward these scale degrees; for example, both the seventh and second scale degrees have a tendency to move toward the first scale degree; the fourth scale degree tends toward the third scale degree, and the sixth scale degree moves toward the fifth scale degree. Most harmonic progressions proceed with the goal of the tonic chord as its finishing chord.

Cadential 6/4

The cadential 6/4 is a specific second inversion chord that tends to appear on weak beats at cadences. The cadential 6/4 chord is an I6/4 that always immediately moves to the dominant chord. It serves as an embellishment of the dominant chord by sharing the bass note of the V chord with the fifth scale degree and by providing smooth voice leading of the first scale degree (tonic) to the seventh scale degree (leading tone) and the fourth scale degree to the third scale degree. When the cadential I6/4 moves to a dominant seventh chord, the voice leading includes the movement of the upper duplicated fifth scale degree descending to the leading tone of the dominant seventh chord.

Pedal 6/4

The pedal 6/4, or the neighboring 6/4, are specific second inversion chords that appear on weak beats providing movement in the upper voices. The names refer to the pedal movement of the bass voices and the neighboring movements of the upper voices in the harmonic progression. The pedal 6/4 is created when the third and fifth notes of a previous chord move up to its neighbor notes in the 6/4 chords and return to the third and fifth notes, while the bass note remains the same. The common pedal 6/4 chords are the I6/4 that appears between two dominant chords in root position and the IV 6/4 chords that appear between two tonic chords in root position.

Passing 6/4

The passing 6/4 refers to a second inversion chord in which the pitches of the chord provide a stepwise movement between the preceding chord and the chord following it. The notes of the passing 6/4 chord fill in the space between the surrounding chords that are usually a third apart. Passing 6/4 chords are commonly found between the I and I^6 chords and the IV and IV^6 chords. The V6/4 chord is used between the I and I6 chords as the bass moves either up or down between the chords, and the I6/4 chord is used between the IV and IV^6 chords. In a passing 6/4 section, the bass and soprano voices exchange voices so that the pitches are inversions of each other. For example, the bass pitches move in a stepwise manner from E-D-C, while the soprano pitches move stepwise from C-D-E.

Arpeggiating 6/4

An arpeggiating 6/4 chord or bass arpeggiating 6/4 chord describes a second inversion chord on a weak beat whose bass note creates a broken chord incidence between the two surrounding chords, while the upper harmony remains the same. This creates movement in the bass line while maintaining the sonority of the upper voices. Any chord can be used as an arpeggiating 6/4 as long as the bass is arpeggiated and the tenor, alto, and soprano pitches hold the same harmony. Some conceivable chord movements include the following: root position tonic moving to an arpeggiating subdominant in second inversion moving back to root position tonic; root position tonic moving to second inversion tonic moving to first inversion tonic; and root position dominant moving to second inversion dominant moving back to root position dominant.

Circle of Fifths

The circle of fifths is a system of organization in which major keys and minor keys are ordered by their number of sharps. Starting from C major, which has zero sharps and flats, the circle of fifths next goes to G major which has one sharp, D major which has two sharps, and so on. The keys are separated by an interval of a fifth, thus the name *circle of fifths*. The minor keys are also separated by an interval of a fifth, for example, a minor that has zero sharps to E minor, which has one sharp.

When five, six and seven sharped keys are reached, enharmonic flat keys are used so that a complete circle is reached, coming back to C major. Keys near each other are generally closely related in terms of functional harmony.

Conclusive and Inconclusive Cadence

A cadence is a combination of chords that make up a closing or ending of a musical section, phrase, or movement. Cadences mark a harmonic, melodic, and rhythmic arrival point in the music. A conclusive cadence refers to a cadence in which the arrival point sounds final. The endings of musical works are most often marked by a conclusive cadence rather than an inconclusive cadence. Conclusive cadences include the perfect authentic cadence, imperfect authentic cadence, and the plagal cadence. An inconclusive cadence refers to a cadence in which the arrival point does not sound final, and something needs to follow it. Inconclusive cadences include the half cadence and deceptive cadence.

Half Cadence and a Phrygian Half Cadence

The half cadence is defined as any harmony progressing to a dominant harmony. The preceding harmony can be the tonic, subdominant, supertonic, or any other harmony. A common half cadence is the tonic in a second inversion resolving to the dominant, notated as $I^6{}_4$--V in Western tonal theory. This particular half cadence is known as the cadential tonic six-four and shares the bass note from the six-four chord with the resulting dominant chord. Oftentimes, the cadential tonic six-four progression occurs at the end of the first section in a two-part or binary piece of music. Other types of half cadences include the Phrygian half cadence, in which a first inversion subdominant chord proceeds to the dominant similarly in the Phrygian mode, and the Lydian half cadence, in which a first inversion subdominant chord is raised by a half step and then resolved to the dominant.

A cadence is a combination of chords that make up a closing or ending of a musical section, phrase, or movement. Cadences mark a harmonic, melodic, and rhythmic arrival point in the music. A half cadence is defined as any cadence that ends on the dominant V or dominant seventh V^7. Preceding chords can include the tonic I, subdominant IV, or the secondary dominant V/V. When the chord preceding the ending dominant V is the minor iv^6 in a minor key, the half cadence is considered to be a Phrygian half cadence, a cadence that stems from modal music. In the Phrygian mode, the final cadential voice leading of the outer voices from a sixth to an octave is preserved in the modern-day Phrygian half cadence.

Authentic Cadence

The authentic cadence is defined as a dominant-sounding harmony resolving to the tonic harmony, notated as V-I or V-i in Western tonal theory. The authentic cadence is considered to be the strongest cadence because of the presence of the supertonic to tonic progression as well as the leading tone to tonic progression. In voice leading, these two progressions exhibit the highest tension and release movements within music theory. An authentic cadence can be either perfect or imperfect. A perfect authentic cadence has both the roots of the V and I chords sounding in the bass and the tonic as the highest-sounding note on the final chord. An imperfect authentic cadence does not involve all the conditions required to be a perfect authentic cadence, and so may not have the tonic sounding in the highest note of the final chord, or may have inverted chords.

Plagal Cadence

The plagal cadence is defined as the subdominant sounding harmony resolving to the tonic harmony, notated as IV-I or iv-i in Western tonal theory. Because there is the absence of a leading tone resolution in a plagal cadence, it is not considered as final or as strong of a cadence as the authentic cadence. Oftentimes, the plagal cadence is found as an extension of an authentic cadence, embellishing the final tonic through the neighboring notes of the third and fourth scale degrees and of the fifth and sixth scale degrees. The plagal cadence is a common ending to many Protestant hymns and is also known as the amen cadence as the cadence is set to the word *amen*. The plagal cadence is so closely associated with Protestant hymns that some composers have used the IV-I progression as an allusion to its sacred usage.

Perfect Authentic Cadence and an Imperfect Authentic Cadence

A cadence is a combination of chords that make up a closing or ending of a musical section, phrase, or movement. Cadences mark a harmonic, melodic, and rhythmic arrival point in the music. The basic authentic cadence is defined as a cadence that moves from the dominant V to the tonic I. Within that classification, there are two subtypes: perfect authentic cadence (PAC) and imperfect authentic cadence (IAC). In PAC, both chords must be in root position with the melody ending on the tonic note. In IAC, the chords are presented in an inverted form, or the melody does not end on the tonic note. Both the PAC and IAC are conclusive cadences.

Musical Texture

Musical texture describes the way that all the various parts and voices of a musical work are combined. Musical aspects of texture include harmony, melody, tempo, timbre, and rhythm. Together, they create specific classifications of texture: monophonic texture describes a single melody line with no harmony or accompaniment; homophonic texture describes a single melody line with an added accompaniment; heterophonic texture describes two or more voices that play lines based on the same melody; and polyphonic texture describes several melodies or parts that are interwoven into a complex whole. Within all of these classifications, texture can also be described as dense if there are many notes per measure or sparse if there are few notes per measure.

Monophony and Homophony

Both monophony and homophony refer to the texture of a musical work. Both textures contain a single main melody line. However, in monophonic texture, there is a single main melodic line with nothing else: no harmony or accompaniment. In homophonic texture, there is a single main melodic line but with added accompaniment. There are two kinds of homophony: chordal homophony and homophony that is melody with a separate accompaniment. In chordal homophony, the texture consists of solid chords in which the soprano line forms the melody, while the alto, tenor, and bass form the accompaniment. In homophony that is melody with a separate accompaniment, the accompaniment can be an Alberti bass, ostinato, separate chords, walking bass, or a countermelody.

Alberti Bass

Alberti bass refers to a style of homophonic accompaniment in which the bass notes consist of repeated broken chords, most often in the pattern of low, high, middle, and high. This accompaniment style was popular in keyboard music of the classical era and is named after Domenico Alberti, an Italian composer and keyboardist who used it extensively. Alberti bass is found commonly in the keyboard music of Haydn, Mozart, and other composers of the time as well as in neoclassical music of the twentieth and twenty-first centuries. This accompaniment pattern provided a continuous flow of notes while providing harmonic structure in homophonic works so that the melody could be clearly delineated.

Walking Bass Pattern

A walking bass pattern describes a bass accompaniment pattern in homophonic music in which the bass notes provide a rhythmically steady pattern of notes that outline the harmony with diatonic tones as well as non-diatonic notes. Walking bass can be in a stepwise movement moving through chord tones as well as non-chord tones. Walking bass can also outline chord tones such as C-E-G-Bb-G-E-C. Walking bass can also alternate between the root and the fifth of a chord. Another example of walking bass patterns includes alternating fourths and fifths in the chord. Walking bass patterns can also use diatonic and chromatic approach tones to other notes within the harmony. Walking bass can also use neighbor groups, that is, the neighbor note above and below the target group in its pattern.

Polyphony

Polyphony refers to the musical texture in which several melodies or parts are interwoven into a complex whole. Each part is able to stand on its own as an independent melody. Imitative polyphony refers to polyphony in which the same musical ideas are used throughout the composition. Imitation is used between the voices as well as in each line. Examples of imitative polyphony include canon in which a melody line is repeated in another part; fugal imitation, in which an entire theme is repeated and developed; and strict imitation, as with Bach's keyboard inventions. Nonimitative polyphony refers to polyphony in which the various melodies or lines do not copy each other but are distinctly different from one another.

Canon and Fugal Imitation

Both canon and fugal imitation are polyphonic textures in which several melodies or parts are interwoven into a complex whole. Each part is able to stand on its own as an independent melody. These two types of polyphony are imitative polyphony, which means that the same musical ideas are used throughout the composition. Imitation is used between the voices as well as in each line. In a canon, each line strictly repeats an extended melody at different times but for the entire duration of the musical work. In fugal imitation, each line repeats the theme but sometimes in a different key as the fugue develops. Fugues contain subjects and countersubjects, whereas canons usually contain only one main extended subject.

Binary Form

Binary form refers to the form of a musical composition in which there are two main contrasting sections of music. Binary forms can be open, meaning that the first section does not end on tonic, or closed, meaning that the first section ends on tonic. Simple binary form describes a musical composition in which the two main contrasting sections of music are of a similar length, usually labeled as AB form. Rounded binary form contains two main contrasting sections, but the beginning musical material returns briefly at the end so that the second section becomes longer than the first. Rounded binary form is usually an open binary form in which the two sections modulate.

Ternary Form

Ternary refers to the form of a musical composition in which there are three sections of music, usually labeled ABA or ABA'. The A section begins in tonic, the B section is in a different key, and the return of the A section is in tonic with or without slight changes. If the return of A is exactly the same, then it is labeled A; if the return of A has been altered, then it is labeled A'. Ternary forms can be open or continuous, meaning that the first section does not end on tonic or closed/sectional, meaning that the first section ends on tonic. The B section usually ends on the dominant V before returning to the beginning material.

Sonata

The sonata refers to a common classical-era composition for solo instruments that has three to four distinct movements. The first movement is usually the allegro in sonata form, also known as sonata allegro form. The second movement is usually adagio in ternary or binary form. The adagio is typically in a different but related key than the first movement, such as the relative minor or the dominant key. The third movement is the scherzo or minuet, and is in ternary form. The key of the third movement is usually in the same key as the first movement. The fourth and final movement of the typical sonata is the allegro or presto in rondo or variation form. The fourth movement is typically in the same key as the first movement.

Sonata Allegro

Sonata allegro refers a form of music usually found as the first movement of a larger sonata work. There are three main sections in sonata allegro form: exposition, development, and recapitulation. The exposition establishes the theme as well as the key of the form and contains the first theme, which is in tonic, and the second theme, which is in the dominant or another related key. The end of the exposition cadences and establishes the new key for the development section. In the development section, the theme is freely manipulated through modulations, or "developed," until the end of the development, when the dominant key is established, signaling a return to the theme in the recapitulation. In the recapitulation, the first and second themes from the exposition reappear but are both in the tonic key this time.

Coda and Codetta

Both the coda and the codetta are found at the ending of a musical section. A coda, however, is usually found at the end of an entire composition and is not made up of the thematic material. A codetta, by contrast, is usually found at the end of the first section in a sonata or ternary form but not at the end of a musical work. A codetta, which literally translated means "little coda," tends to be shorter and more minor in its appearance. A coda is usually longer and has a more major presence at the end of a composition. Both a coda and a codetta serve to reinforce the cadence at the end in its finality.

Structure of Vocal Music

Vocal music generally contains verses and choruses. Verses refer to the section of music that contains the same melody but has different lyrics for each verse of the song. Verses can also be known as stanzas and tend to be the section where the story is told. A chorus contains the same lyrics every time it is sung and is typically found between the verses. Another name for the chorus is the refrain. Some vocal works contain features such as an introduction, a bridge, a break, and an outro. A song introduction is a brief musical segment that comes at the beginning of the song, whereas an outro is a brief musical segment that ends the song. A bridge is usually placed two thirds of the way through a song to provide contrasting musical material. A break often features instrumental solos.

Strophic and Through-Composed Music

Strophic music refers to vocal music in which the verses of the text are sung to the same melody and is the simpler form. Through-composed music refers to vocal music in which each verse has a different melody and tends to be more complex. In through-composed music, the music feels much more continuous without clear verse breaks, as in strophic music, and has more of a sense of musical as well as lyrical development. Strophic music tends to feel more repetitive because the melody is repeated in each verse. Popular vocal music tends to use the strophic form, whereas art music tends to use the through-composed form.

Antiphon and Antiphonal Music

An antiphon refers to the call-and-response style often used in sacred religious settings. The text to the call and response can either be sung or spoken so that every call is followed by a response from the choir or the congregation. The text is derived from a psalm, a musical work, other religious writing, or Gregorian chant. Antiphonal music stems from the antiphon and refers to a call-and-response style of singing in which two choirs or two sections of the choir alternate parts so that the effect is still a call and response. Antiphonal music can also be described as polychoral music because two groups of singers sing alternating parts within the same work.

Terrace Dynamics

Terraced dynamics refers to sectional dynamic changes that occur apart from the gradual dynamic changes that occur with crescendo and decrescendo. For example, a terraced dynamic from soft to loud would occur this way—*pp, p, mp, mf, f, ff*—as sudden, dynamic shifts. Terraced dynamics from loud to soft would occur as follows: *ff, f, mf, mp, p*, and *pp*. This practice stems from the Baroque era in which gradual dynamic changes were not common abilities of most of the era instruments. Many keyboard instruments made dynamic changes through the addition of strings, as in the harpsichord, or changing of manuals or adding additional pipes, as in the organ, and required the operation of a stop. Baroque ensembles performed dynamic changes by adding or subtracting instruments that doubled the musical line.

Dynamic Markings Commonly Used in Music

The dynamic markings commonly used in music come from the written Italian musical tradition of the 17th century. In order of increasing loudness, *pianissimo*, abbreviated *pp*, indicates that the player should play very soft. *Piano*, abbreviated *p*, indicates that the player should play soft. *Mezzo piano*, abbreviated *mp*, indicates that the player should play moderately soft. *Mezzo forte*, abbreviated *mf*, indicates that the player should play moderately loud. *Forte*, abbreviated *f*, indicates that the player should play loud. *Fortissimo*, abbreviated *ff*, indicates that the player should play very loud. Dynamic markings that indicate a gradual change include crescendo and decrescendo or diminuendo. A crescendo indicates that the player should play increasingly louder. A decrescendo or diminuendo indicates that the player should play increasingly softer.

Manipulating Stringed Instruments

On a stringed instrument, many techniques can be applied to produce dynamic changes. When playing with a bow, the variables that affect dynamics are speed and pressure of the bow. When playing louder dynamics such as *forte*, *fortissimo*, and *mezzo forte*, the bow must move faster across the strings with greater pressure to produce greater amplitudes in the vibrating sound waves. When playing softer dynamics such as *piano*, *mezzo piano*, and *pianissimo*, the bow most a little slower across the strings with less pressure to produce smaller amplitudes in the vibrating sound waves. When stringed instruments are plucked, this is often notated in the score as *pizzicato*. When plucking a stringed instrument, the sound produced has a sharper attack; dynamic changes are produced similarly: a heavier pluck at greater speed increases dynamics, whereas a softer, slower pluck diminishes the dynamics.

Change in Tempo

The terms *affretando*, *slentando*, *allargando*, and *calando* all direct the musician to produce a change in tempo. *Affretando* comes from the Italian word *affretare*, which means "to hurry." When notated within musical notation, *affretando* indicates a quickening of the tempo and also a character or mood of agitation. *Slentando* comes from the Italian word *slentare*, which means "to slow down." The player should gradually decrease the tempo of the section as the music slows down. *Allargando* comes from the Italian word *allargare*, which means "to widen." In music, the player should gradually decrease the tempo in a deliberate and imposing character. *Calando* comes from the Italian word *calare*, which means "to let down." Musically, the player should gradually decrease both the tempo and the volume as *calando* indicates a mood of calming and dying away.

Tempo Markings in Order from Slowest to Fastest

These tempo markings in order from slowest to fastest are: *larghissimo, largo, larghetto, andante, moderato, allegro, vivace,* and *presto. Larghissimo* comes from the Italian meaning "very or extremely broad" and should be played very slowly. *Largo* comes from the Italian meaning "broad" and should be played slowly. *Larghetto* is slightly faster than *largo. Andante* comes from the Italian meaning "in a walking manner" and should be played slightly faster than *adagio* but slower than *moderato. Moderato* comes from the Italian meaning "moderately" and should be played at an easy, comfortable pace. *Allegro* comes from the Italian meaning "fast" and should be played at a quick tempo. *Vivace* comes from the Italian meaning "lively" and should be played faster than allegro but slower than *presto. Presto* comes from the Italian meaning "very fast" and should be played very quickly.

Pitch Duration

Articulation markings can range from those indicating a shortening of pitch duration to those indicating a lengthening of pitch duration. These articulation markings are presented in decreasing order of duration length: *tenuto, portato, staccato,* and *staccatissimo. Tenuto,* from the Italian word *tenere,* meaning "to hold," directs the player to hold the note for its full value. In musical notation, a horizontal line over or under the note head marks the tenuto. *Portato,* from the Italian word *portare,* meaning "to carry," directs the player to smoothly detach the notes similarly to a *legato* but shorter in length and longer than a *staccato.* Both dots and a slur over or under the note heads mark the *portato. Staccato,* from the Italian word *staccare,* meaning "to detach," directs the player to shortly detach the note. A dot over or under the note head marks the *staccato. Staccatissimo* is an extremely shortened note and is notated by a wedge or pike above or under the note head.

Con Amore, Con Bravura, Con Brio, Con Fuoco, Con Grazia, and Con Tenerezza

Con, "with," indicates each of these terms as descriptions or instructions of a performer's phrasing. *Con amore* translates to "with love" and is equivalent to *amorevole* or *amoroso,* "lovingly." *Con amore* may have multiple correlates within the performance style, translating into a *legato* articulation, *rubato,* and more dramatic dynamic contrast. *Con bravura,* similarly, translates to "with bravery" and is a different connotation from *bravura* as in a *bravura* performance, which means "skill"; *con brio,* or *brioso,* "with spirit"; *con fuoco,* "with fire"; *con grazia,* "with grace"; or *con tenerezza,* "with tenderness." Each term is somewhat subjective; indeed, it may be difficult to establish clear distinctions among *con amore, con tenerezza,* and *con grazia,* for example, and will result in similar interpretations. *Con brioso, con fuoco,* and *con bravura* also have many characteristics in common and will differ from an *amoroso* performance that would have more staccato articulations and limited *rubato.*

Forzando (z), Rinforzando (rinf), and Sforzando (sfz)

The dynamic markings *forzando* (*z*), *rinforzando* (*rinf*), and *sforzando* (*sfz*) all refer to an increased loudness in sound. All three Italian directives have roots from the Italian word *forzare,* which means "to force." *Forzando,* meaning forced, directs the musician to strongly accent the notes over which the marking occurs. *Rinforzando,* however, has an added prefix and means more precisely "reinforcing" or "strengthening." The *rinf* dynamic marking usually refers to the increase in volume of a group of notes throughout a phrase and is played increasingly louder similarly to a *cresc* but over a shorter length of time. *Sforzando* is most similar to *forzando,* and the two terms can be interchanged to mean a sudden increase in loudness of the note or notes over which the marking occurs.

Notational Skills

Grand Staff

When notating a grand staff, several key elements must be included. First, the grand staff must include the treble clef as well as the bass clef; each clef has five lines and four spaces. The two clefs are connected by a line down the side to the left as well as a brace. Subsequent measures are notated by a full line extending from the top of the treble clef down to the bottom of the bass clef. To the right of the clef symbols, the key signature must be notated in each clef, whether in sharps or flats. Next is the time signature, which must also be notated in each clef. The time signature is only notated once at the beginning of the musical work; the key signature must be notated at the beginning of each line.

Musical Symbols

Rhythm is the movement of music over time. As such, certain musical aspects, such as pitch duration, silence, and meter, play key roles in translating musical symbols to real-time musical rhythm. Pitch durations are notated through note values that sound for a specified time. Whole notes are held through four quarter-note lengths. Half notes are held through two quarter-note lengths. Quarter notes are held for half the length of a half note. Eighth notes are held for half the length of a quarter note. Sixteenth notes are held for half the length of an eighth note, and so forth. Silence durations are notated through rests, which have note name equivalents; that is, whole notes and whole rests both have durations of four quarter-note lengths. Meters are essential in establishing rhythm as meters define the general organization of stresses and pulses.

Rhythmic Pattern Examples

Augmentation

<u>Rewrite the following rhythmic pattern using augmentation.</u>

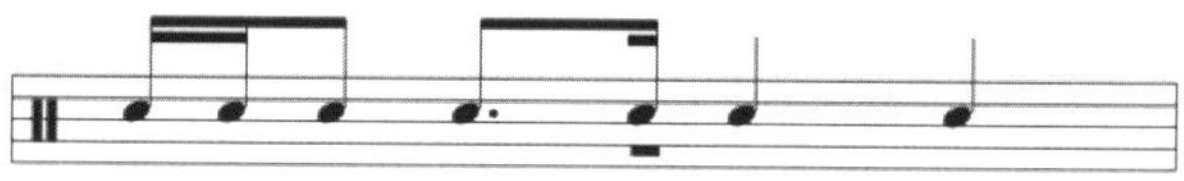

To augment a rhythm, rhythmic values are generally doubled. In the example, sixteenth notes should become eighth notes, eighth notes should become quarter notes, and quarter notes should become half notes. So, instead of two sixteenths to start the excerpt, now two eighth notes start the excerpt. The next two note values are variants of eighth notes and are now augmented to become a quarter note followed by a dotted quarter note. The next sixteenth becomes an eighth note, and the last two quarter notes become two half notes.

Diminution

<u>Rewrite the following rhythmic pattern using diminution.</u>

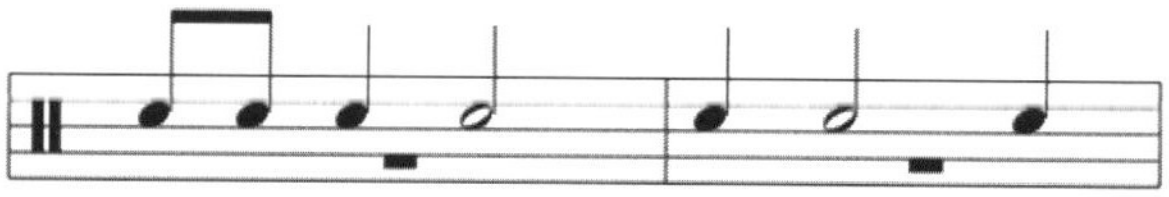

Rhythmic diminution involves rewriting the note values in smaller values, usually half of their original rhythmic value. In the example, eighth notes should become sixteenths, quarter notes should become half notes, and half notes should become quarter notes. The excerpt begins with two eighth notes that through diminution are now are sixteenth notes. The quarters and half notes that follow become eighth note and quarter note values.

Supply Missing Note Examples

Example 1

Write in the missing note value at the end of the following rhythmic example.

In the compound 9/8 time signatures, there should be nine eighth notes or three groups of three eighth notes. Two sixteenth notes together make one eighth note value. In the example, the first two sixteenth notes together make one eighth note; the following two eighth notes make the first of three groups of three eighth notes. The next group contains a dotted eighth note, which accounts for one and a half eighth notes, plus the next three sixteenth notes, which also equal one and a half eighth notes; together these make up the second group of three eighth notes. The last group contains only a quarter note, which equals two eighth notes. Therefore, the missing note value is one eighth note.

Example 2

5/4 meter: Write the missing note value at the end of the following rhythmic example.

In 5/4 time signatures, there should be five quarter notes. There are two eighth notes in a quarter note value and two sixteenth notes in an eighth-note value. In the example, the first beat has the sixteenth rest plus the next sixteenth and eighth note. The next beat has the sixteenth, eighth, and tied sixteenth note.

The third beat is also present with the tied dotted eighth note and sixteenth note. The fourth beat has the eighth note plus the two sixteenth notes. The fifth beat is not present; therefore, the missing note is a quarter note.

Example 3

4/2 meter: Write the missing note value at the end of the following rhythmic example.

In 4/2 time signatures, there should be four half notes. There are two quarter notes in a half note value, two eighth notes in a quarter note, and two sixteenth notes in an eighth note. In the example, the first quarter note plus the dotted eighth and sixteenth together make up the first beat. The next beat has the two sixteenth notes, the eighth rest, and the next quarter note. The third beat has the quarter note and the two eighth notes. The fourth beat has the two sixteenth notes and the two tied eighth notes. However, this makes up three quarters of the beat. The last quarter is half of a quarter note, which is an eighth note. Therefore, the missing note is an eighth note.

Relationship Among Eighth, Sixteenth, Thirty-Second, and Sixty-Fourth Notes

Eighth notes, sixteenth notes, thirty-second notes, and sixty-fourth notes are all related as subdivisions of each other. Eighth notes have one flag; sixteenth notes have two flags; thirty-second notes have three flags; and sixty-fourth notes have four flags. With each addition of a flag to the note, the note value is halved. For example, there are two eighth notes in a quarter note, or each eighth note is half of a quarter note. For each eighth note, there are two thirty-second notes, or each thirty-second note is half the value of an eighth note. For each thirty-second note, there are two sixty-fourth notes, or each sixty-fourth note is half the value of a thirty-second note.

Common Time and Cut Time

Common time refers to the time signature 4/4 with four beats per measure, with the quarter note receiving the beat. Common time is notated by the symbol C. Cut time refers to the time signature 2/2 with two beats per measure, with the half note receiving the beat. Cut time is also known as cut common time or by the Italian term *alla breve*, which translates to "in the style of the breve." The breve is a double whole note, a value twice the value of a whole note. Cut time generally indicates a quicker tempo in which the overall rhythmic pulse of the piece can be felt in two, as opposed to four, as in common time.

Identifying the Counting Patterns

Example 1

Identify the counting pattern for the following rhythmic example.

In the rhythmic example in common time, each beat is assigned a number 1 through 4 starting, with 1 as the first beat. Each sixteenth note subdivision follows the pattern 1e&a for each sixteenth note in a beat.

Example 2

Identify the counting pattern for the following rhythmic example.

In the rhythmic example in compound duple, each beat is assigned a number 1 through 6, starting with 1 as the first beat. Each sixteenth note subdivision follows the pattern 1& for each sixteenth note in a beat.

Irregular and Asymmetrical Meters

Irregular or asymmetrical meters refer to a time signature that does not have an even number other than three on top and can be subdivided into two unequal groups of notes. For example, in a time signature of 5/4, the quarter notes can be divided into three and two, or two and three, or asymmetrical groups. The pulse pattern is also uneven with metrical accents on the first and fourth beats or on the first and third beats. In a time signature of 7/4, the quarter notes can be divided into four and three or three and four. Occasionally, the groups will be divided into two, two, and three or three, two, and two. The resultant pulse pattern then creates metrical stresses on every first and fifth beats or on every first and fourth beats.

Polyrhythm and Cross Rhythm

Polyrhythm refers to a rhythm that uses two distinctly different patterns at the same time. Polyrhythms can occur as a continuous pattern throughout a musical work or as a momentary rhythmic disruption in a musical work. For example, a rhythmic pattern of straight quarter notes played alongside a highly syncopated samba rhythm would be considered a polyrhythm. Another example of a polyrhythm would be constant triplets over constant duplets. A cross rhythm is a specific type of polyrhythm coined by early ethnomusicologists studying African rhythms. Common cross rhythmic ratios include the following: three against two, six against four, three against four, three against eight, and four against three.

Swing Rhythm

Swing rhythm is often notated with straight eighth notes with an instructional note for the eighth notes to be "swing." Occasionally, the swing rhythm will be notated with a quarter note followed by an eighth note under a triplet symbol to be played within a triplet rhythm. When performed, the eighth notes are played as the first and third notes of a triplet to create a rhythmic swinging feel of a long-short rhythmic pattern. The first note of a swing rhythm should be twice as long as the second note in a medium swing rhythm in a ratio of two to one. In a hard swing rhythm, the music should be played as a dotted eighth note followed by a sixteenth note so that the ratio is three to one. Light swing or shuffle rhythm consists of a longer eighth note followed by a shorter eighth note in an approximate ratio of three to two.

Alto Clef

The alto clef uses a C clef on the third line of the staff to indicate where the C4 pitch is located. The middle part of the symbol points to the C pitch. The pitches for the five lines starting from the bottom line are F, A, C, E, and G; the pitches for the four spaces starting with the bottom space are G, B, D, and F. Other names for the alto clef are the viola clef, because it is the usual clef used in viola music notation, and the countertenor clef, because it is often used in countertenor music notation. Other instruments that use the alto clef are the viola da gamba, the mandola, the alto trombone, the cor anglais, and occasionally the piano.

Treble Clef

The treble clef uses a G clef on the second line of the staff to indicate where the G4 pitch is located. The curl of the symbol circles around the line to indicate the G pitch. The pitches for the five lines starting from the bottom line are E, G, B, D, and F; the pitches for the four spaces starting with the bottom space are F, A, C, and E. The treble clef is the most common clef used in current music notation. Instruments that use the treble clef include the piano, the soprano voice, the violin, the trumpet, the horn, the flute, the vibraphone, the guitar, the oboe, the euphonium, and many others. The treble clef is also used in conjunction with the bass clef to create the grand staff.

Bass Clef

The bass clef uses an F clef on the fourth line of the staff to indicate where the F3 pitch is located. The two dots of the symbol surround the line where the F3 pitch is located. The pitches of the five lines starting from the bottom line are G, B, D, F, and A; the pitches for the four spaces starting with the bottom space are A, C, E, and G. The bass clef is one of the more common clefs in use today, along with the treble clef. Instruments that use the bass clef include the piano, the bass, the bassoon, the trombone, the tuba, the timpani, the cello, the bass voice, and many others. The bass clef is also used in conjunction with the treble clef to create the grand staff.

Tenor Clef

The tenor clef uses a C clef on the fourth line of the staff to indicate where the C4 pitch is located. The middle part of the symbol points to the C pitch. The pitches for the five lines starting from the bottom line are D, F, A, C, and E; the pitches for the four spaces starting with the bottom space are E, G, B, and D. Instruments that use the tenor clef include the cello, the bassoon, the trombone, the euphonium, the tenor violin, and the double bass. The tenor clef was previously used for the tenor voice, but current usage has the treble clef with an octave lower indication for the tenor voice or the bass clef.

G-Clef, the C-Clef, and the F-Clef

All clefs indicate the position of a particular pitch on the five-lined staff. The G-clef, the C-clef, and the F-clef are the most common clefs used in modern Western music notation. The G-clef spirals around the second line from the bottom, indicating it as the G line for the G pitch above middle C. The C-clef has a middle point that is placed to indicate the line as middle C. The C-clef can be placed on the third line, in which it is typically called the alto or viola clef; when it is placed on the fourth line from the bottom, it is typically called the tenor clef. The F-clef looks somewhat like a backwards C with two dots to the right of it; the top point of the curve is placed on the fourth line from the bottom so that the two dots also surround the same line, indicating it as the F pitch below middle C.

Stem Rule

The stem rule when notating pitches refers to the direction and placement of note stems. When a note is placed below the third line of the staff, the stem is drawn on the right side of the note extending up. When the note is placed on the third line or above, the stem is drawn on the left side of the note extending down. The note head and stem is always the same when manipulated and can be thought of as right side up or upside down. The stem should extend roughly three space lengths. This rule applies with ledger lines as well as the decisive measure is still the third line on any staff.

Four Main Clefs Commonly Used in Orchestral Writing

The four main clefs commonly used in orchestral writing are the treble, alto, tenor, and bass clefs. The treble clef, also known as the G-clef, is shaped so that the spiral of the symbol circles the G-line on the staff. The instruments that typically employ the treble clef include the violin, woodwinds, high basses, and the treble range of keyboard instruments. The alto clef, also known as the C-clef, is shaped so that the middle point of the symbol rests on the third line as middle C. The instrument that typically employs the alto clef is the viola. The tenor clef also uses the C-clef but is placed so that the middle point of the symbol rests on the fourth line as middle C. Instruments that sometimes use the tenor clef include the cello, bassoon, and trombone. The bass clef, also known as the F-clef, is shaped so that two dots of the symbol surround the F-line. Instruments that typically employ the bass clef include the double bass, cello, bassoon, trombone, low brasses, and the bass range of keyboard instruments.

Accidentals

Accidentals are used in music notation to indicate an alteration to the specific pitch that it is in front of. The five accidentals are the natural sign, the sharp, the flat, the double flat, and the double sharp. A natural sign in front of a note indicates that any previously flatted or sharped note should be canceled and the pitch should be played without alteration. A sharp sign in front of a note indicates that the pitch should be played a half step higher. A flat sign in front of a note indicates that the pitch should be played a half step lower. A double flat symbol in front of a note indicates that the pitch should be played two half steps lower. A double sharp symbol in front of a note indicates that the pitch should be played two half steps higher.

Clef and Notation Examples

Alto Clef Example

Notate the alto clef and a whole note on C4 and explain.

The alto clef uses the C clef, which has two curves that meet in the center and two lines to the left of it. The point where the curves meet is C4. For the alto clef, the C clef rests on the third line; therefore, C4 is the third line of the staff.

Treble Clef Example

Notate the treble clef and a whole note on C4 and explain.

The treble clef uses the G clef, which has a line that curls around, over, and down. The line where the curl originates marks G4, thus the name for the G clef. The distance from G4 down to C4 is an interval of a fifth. C4 on the treble clef requires one ledger line below the staff to mark C4.

Bass Clef Example

Notate the bass clef and a whole note on C4 and explain.

The bass clef uses the F clef, which has a dot on the F3 line and wraps downward around it; two dots to the right surround the F3 line. The distance from F3 to C4 is an interval of a fifth upward. C4 on the bass clef requires one ledger line above the staff to mark C4.

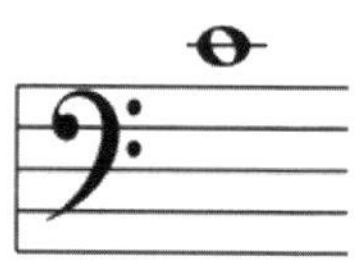

Tenor Clef Example

Notate the tenor clef and a whole note on C4 and explain.

The tenor clef uses the C clef, which has two curves that meet in the center and two lines to the left of it. The point where the curves meet is C4. For the tenor clef, the C clef rests on the fourth line from the bottom; therefore, C4 is the fourth line of the staff.

Enharmonic Equivalents

Enharmonic equivalents refer to the nomenclature phenomenon that occurs on any pitch, interval, or chord that can be labeled with more than one name. For example, C# can also be labeled as Db, even though it is the same identical pitch, and is called its enharmonic note. Enharmonic intervals indicate different labeling of the same pitches. For example, the interval of an augmented fourth C to F# can also be labeled as a diminished fifth, if it is relabeled as C to Gb. Similarly, enharmonic chords use different labels on the same harmonies. A B major chord, B – D# – F#, has an enharmonic equivalent of Cb major when spelled Cb – Eb – Gb. Certain scales have enharmonic equivalents as well, such as the C# major scale and the Db major scale.

Key Signature

The key signature is the set of sharps or flats at the beginning of a musical work that designates the key or tonal center of the music. The accidentals at the beginning of the piece, usually found immediately after the clef symbols and before the time signature, apply to every pitch in the piece and not that specific tone. For example, if there is a sharp on the F5 pitched line in the key signature, all Fs will be sharped and not just the F5. There are twelve common diatonic key signatures that are most used, along with their minor keys. Major keys have relative minor keys that share the same key signature. To find the relative minor key for a specific major key, go down three half steps to find the relative minor key. For example, the relative minor key to C major is a minor, three half steps below C.

Order of Sharps in a Key Signature

In current Western musical tradition, there is a specific ordering of the sharps in a key signature directly related to the circle of fifths. The order of sharps in a key signature follows the circle of fifths clockwise in which keys are separated by the rising interval of a fifth, with each successive key containing an additional sharp. For example, C major has zero sharps. An interval of a fifth above would be G major with one sharp; a fifth above that would be D major with two sharps. Therefore, the order would also follow that the first sharp is the sharp within G major, the second sharp would be the one added to D major, and so on. Each sharp that is added acts as the leading tone to the key. The order of sharps, then, is F, C, G, D, A, E, and B.

Order of Flats in a Key Signature

In current Western musical tradition, there is a specific ordering of the flats in a key signature directly related to the circle of fifths. The order of flats in a key signature follows the circle of fifths counterclockwise in which keys are separated by the falling interval of a fifth, with each successive key containing an additional flat. For example, C major has zero sharps. An interval of a fifth below would be F major with one flat; a fifth below that would be Bb major with two flats. Therefore, the order would also follow that the first flat is the flat within F major, the second flat would be the one added to Bb major, and so on. Each flat that is added acts as the subdominant of the key. The order of flats, then, is B, E, A, D, G, C, and F.

Tonality of a Sharp Major Key Signature

When given an excerpt of music with a sharp key signature from which to identify the major key, there are two ways to determine the key. In the first method, the order of the circle of fifths is central to identifying the key signature. Take into account the number of sharps, and that is the number of turns clockwise around the circle of fifths. For example, to figure out a key signature that contains five sharps, take five turns around the circle of fifths starting with C—1:G, 2:D, 3:A, 4:E, and 5:B—and the fifth turn is the key that contains five sharps. The other method involves the relationship of the last sharp as the leading tone to the key. Take the last sharp in the key signature;

raise it by a half step to find the major key. For example, in the key signature that has the last sharp as D#, a half step up finds the key as E major.

Tonality of a Flat Major Key Signature

When given an excerpt of music with a flat key signature from which to identify the major key, there are two ways to determine the key. In the first method, the order of the circle of fifths is central to identifying the key signature. Take into account the number of flats, and that is the number of turns counterclockwise around the circle of fifths. For example, to figure out a key signature that contains four flats, take four turns counterclockwise around the circle of fifths starting with C—1:F, 2:Bb, 3:Eb, and 4:Ab—and the fourth turn is the key that contains four flats. The other method involves the relationship of the last flat as subdominant to the key. Take the penultimate flat, and that is the key signature because each added flat is a fourth apart. For example, in the key signature that has the last two flats as Eb and Ab, the next-to-last flat is Eb, so the key is in Eb (Ab is the subdominant of Eb major).

Key Signature Examples

Eb Major Key

Write the Eb major key signature and explain.

The order of flats for the flat key signatures is always Bb, Eb, Ab, Db, Gb, C, and Fb. To find the number of flats in Eb major, the number of turns counterclockwise around the circle of fifths is the same number of flats in the key signature. Starting on C (0), down a fifth is F (1), down another fifth is Bb (2), and down another fifth is Eb (3); so, the key of Eb major has three flats: Bb, Eb, and Ab.

A Major Key

Write the A major key signature and explain.

The order of sharps for the sharp key signatures is always F#, C#, G#, D#, A#, E#, and B#. To find the number of sharps in A major, the number of turns clockwise around the circle of fifths is the same number of sharps in the key signature. Starting on C (0), up a fifth is G (1), up another fifth is D (2), and up another fifth is A (3); so, the key of A major has three sharps: F#, C#, and G#.

C# Major Key

Write the C# major key signature and explain.

The order of sharps for the sharp key signatures is always F#, C#, G#, D#, A#, E#, and B#. To find the number of sharps in C# major, the number of turns clockwise around the circle of fifths is the same number of sharps in the key signature. Starting on C (0), up a fifth is G (1), up another fifth is D (2), up another fifth is A (3), up another fifth is E (4), up another fifth is B (5), up another fifth is F# (6), and up another fifth is C# (7); so, the key of C# major has seven sharps: F#, C#, G#, D#, A#, E#, and B#.

Bb Major Key

Write the Bb major key signature and explain.

The order of flats for the flat key signatures is always Bb, Eb, Ab, Db, Gb, C, and Fb. To find the number of flats in Bb major, the number of turns counterclockwise around the circle of fifths is the same number of flats in the key signature. Starting on C (0), down a fifth is F (1), and down another fifth is Bb (2); so, the key of Bb major has two flats: Bb and Eb.

E MINOR KEY

WRITE THE E MINOR KEY SIGNATURE AND EXPLAIN.

The order of sharps for the sharp key signatures is always F#, C#, G#, D#, A#, E#, and B#. To find the number of sharps in E minor, the number of turns clockwise around the minor circle of fifths is the same number of sharps in the key signature. Starting on A minor (0), up a fifth is E (1); so, the key of E minor has one sharp: F#.

BB MINOR KEY

WRITE THE BB MINOR KEY SIGNATURE AND EXPLAIN.

The order of flats for the flat key signatures is always Bb, Eb, Ab, Db, Gb, C, and Fb. To find the number of flats in Bb minor, the number of turns counterclockwise around the minor circle of fifths is the same number of flats in the key signature. Starting on A minor (0), down a fifth is D (1), down another fifth is G (2), down another fifth is C (3), down another fifth is F (4), and down another fifth is Bb (5); so, the key of Bb minor has five flats: Bb, Eb, Ab, Db, and Gb.

C# MINOR KEY

WRITE THE C# MINOR KEY SIGNATURE AND EXPLAIN.

The order of sharps for the sharp key signatures is always F#, C#, G#, D#, A#, E#, and B#. To find the number of sharps in C# minor, the number of turns clockwise around the minor circle of fifths is the same number of sharps in the key signature. Starting on A minor (0), up a fifth is E (1), up another fifth is B (2), up another fifth is F# (3), and up another fifth is C# (4); so, the key of C# minor has four sharps: F#, C#, G#, and D#.

A Minor Key

Write the A minor key signature and explain.

To find the key signature for A minor, keep in mind the relative major key to A minor. From A, go up three half steps to find C major, the relative major key. Both A minor and its relative C major are the starting points for the minor and major circle of fifths, respectively. Because they are the starting keys, neither have any sharps or flats. Therefore, the key signature for A minor is zero sharps or flats.

Parallel and Relative Keys

Major and minor keys can be related in one of two ways: parallel relationships and relative relationships. Parallel key relationships are keys that share the same tonic note. For example, the key of F major has a parallel key relationship to F minor because they share the same tonic despite the difference of their modes. Relative key relationships are keys that share the same key signature. For example, both E major and C# minor share the same key signature of four sharps. Relative keys are always separated by three half steps and are closely related keys in terms of harmonic modulations. To find the relative minor for a major key, descend three semitones to find the tonic of the minor key.

Minor Key from a Key Signature

When given an excerpt of music with a key signature from which to identify the minor key, there are two ways to determine the key. In the first method, the order of the minor circle of fifths is central to identifying the key signature. Take into account the number of sharps, and that is the number of turns around the minor circle of fifths. For example, to figure out a key signature that contains three sharps, take three turns around the circle of fifths starting with A—1:E, 2:B, and 3:F#—and the third turn is the minor key that contains three sharps. The other method involves the relationship of the last sharp as supertonic to the minor key. Take the last sharp in the key signature; lower it by a whole step to find the key. For example, for the key signature that has the last sharp as D#, a whole step down finds the key as C# minor.

Circle of Fifths

The circle of fifths describes the relationship and pattern of major and minor keys from one to the next as they move up or down in fifths. Moving up a fifth from C becomes G; moving up a fifth from

G becomes D; moving up a fifth from D becomes A, and so on. The circle of fifths is modeled so that eventually, with enharmonic naming, it goes through all twelve keys back to C. As each key moves along the circle, a sharp or flat is added depending on the direction of the circle. For example, the key of C major has zero flats; moving down a fifth, F major has one flat; moving down another fifth, Bb has two flats, and so on. The circle of fifths can be applied to both major keys and to minor keys and is also useful in determining the degree of relatedness among keys.

Determining Which Accidentals to Use for a Given Mode

When determining which accidentals to use for a given mode, it is important to remember the relationship of modes to the white keys of a keyboard: Ionian starts on C, Dorian starts on D, Phrygian starts on E, Lydian starts on F, Mixolydian starts on G, Aeolian starts on A, and Locrian starts on B. With these relationships in mind, a simple formula can be used in which the key signature to use for a given mode corresponds to its distance above C: Dorian a M2, Phrygian a M3, Lydian a P4, Mixolydian a P5, Aeolian an M6, and Locrian an M7. The mode then will use the key signature of the key that is a major third, for example, below the starting note. For example, to find the accidentals for a Lydian mode starting on A, go down a perfect fourth to get the key of E major. Write the mode starting on A while using the four sharps of E major – F#, C#, G#, ad D#.

C Ionian Mode

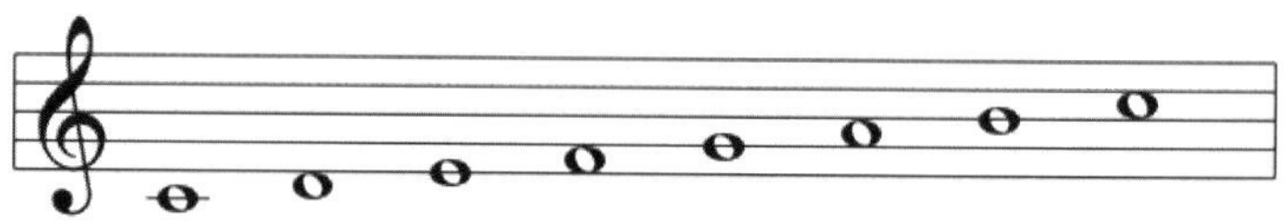

The Ionian mode describes the major scale series, having the following intervals: whole step (W) half step (H), W, W, W, and H. In the key of C, the Ionian mode produces the scale shown in this measure: C, D, E, F, G, A, B, and C.

C Dorian Mode

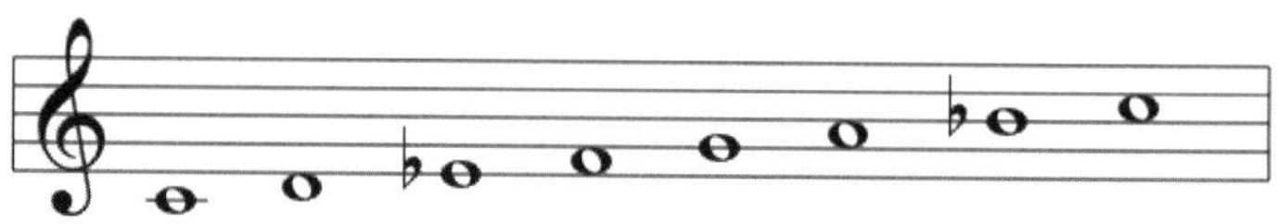

The Dorian mode describes a scale series having the following intervals: whole step (W), half step (H), W, W, W, H, and W. In the key of C, the Dorian mode produces the scale shown in this measure: C, D, Eb, F, G, A, Bb, and C.

C Phrygian Mode

The Phrygian mode describes a scale series having the following intervals: half step (H), whole step (W), W, W, H, W, and W. In the key of C, the Phrygian mode produces the scale shown in this measure: C, Db, Eb, F, G, Ab, Bb, and C.

C Lydian Mode

The Lydian mode describes a scale series having the following intervals: whole step (W), W, W, half step (H), W, W, and H. In the key of C, the Lydian mode produces the scale shown in this measure: C, D, E, F#, G, A, B, and C.

C Mixolydian Mode

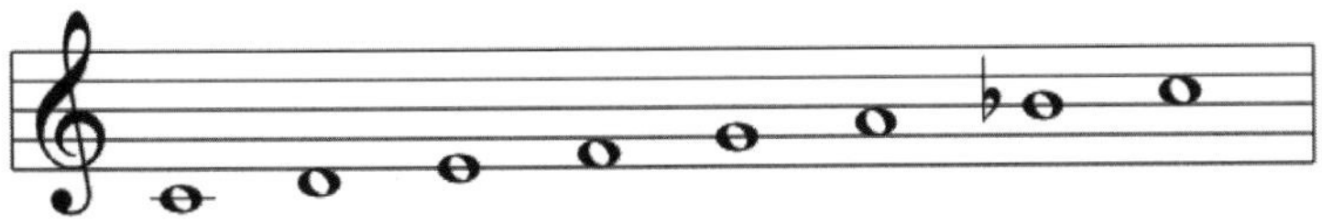

The Mixolydian mode describes a scale series having the following intervals: whole step (W), W, half step (H), W, W, H, and W. In the key of C, the Mixolydian mode produces the scale shown in this measure: C, D, E, F, G, A, Bb, and C.

C Aeolian Mode

The Aeolian mode describes the minor scale series having the following intervals: whole step (W), half step (H), W, W, H, W, and W. In the key of C, the Aeolian mode produces the scale shown in this measure: C, D, Eb, F, G, Ab, Bb, and C.

C Locrian Mode

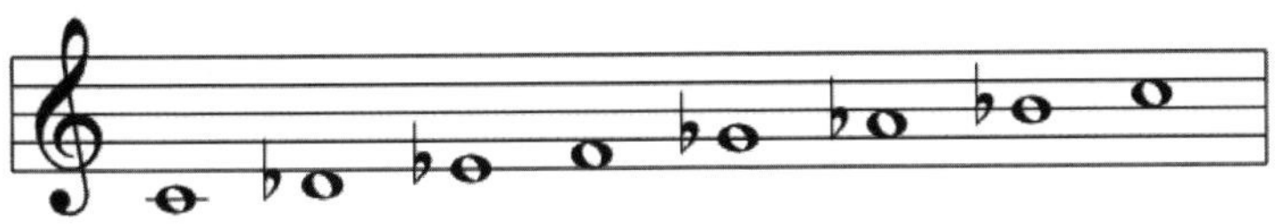

The Locrian mode describes a scale series having the following intervals: half step (H), whole step (W), W, H, W, W, and W. In the key of C, the Locrian mode produces the scale shown in this measure: C, Db, Eb, F, Gb, Ab, Bb, and C.

Interval of a Major Fourteenth Above C4

C4 indicates middle C. To find the pitch that is a major fourteenth above middle C, count fourteen lines and spaces above middle C, starting with one on middle C. Another method is to subtract seven from fourteen, which gives seven. A seventh above middle C is B, so a fourteenth would be the B an octave above, or B5.

Interval of an Augmented Fourth Below B4

B4 indicates the B above middle C. To find the pitch that is an augmented fourth below B4, first go down four lines and spaces to F4 to make the interval of a fourth. Next, make any alterations necessary to make the quality of the interval augmented. In this case, natural F4 is already an augmented interval to B4.

Interval of a Perfect 8ve Above E4

E4 indicates E above middle C. To find the pitch that is a perfect 8ve above E4, count eight lines and spaces above E4 starting with one on E4. Another method is to find the same letter name an octave higher, hence the 8ve designation, to find E5.

Interval of a Minor Sixth Above D3

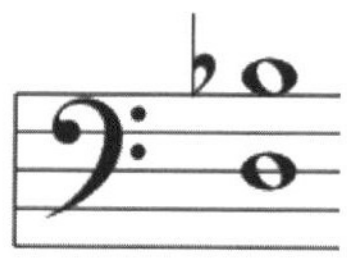

D3 indicates the D below middle C. To find the pitch that is a minor sixth above D3, first count six lines and spaces above D3 starting with one on D3 to make the interval of a sixth. Next, make any alterations necessary to make the quality of the interval minor. Because the minor sixth exists as the sixth scale degree in D minor scale, simply find the key signature—one flat on B—to make the note Bb3.

Interval of a Diminished Seventh Above C3

C3 indicates bass clef C. To find the pitch that is a diminished seventh above C3, first count seven lines and spaces above C3, starting with one on C3, to make the interval of a seventh. Next, make any alterations necessary to make the quality of the diminished interval. Because C to B is a major interval, the pitch must be lowered by two semitones to the note Bbb3 to make the interval of a diminished seventh.

Interval of an Augmented Third Above F4

F4 indicates the F above middle C. To find the pitch that is an augmented third above F4, first count three lines and spaces above to find the interval of a third, starting with one on F4. Next, make any alterations necessary to make the quality of the augmented interval. Because F to A is a major interval, the pitch must be raised by a semitone to the note A# to make the interval of an augmented third.

Interval of a Perfect Eleventh Above C3

C3 indicates bass clef C. To find the pitch that is a perfect eleventh above C3, first count eleven lines and spaces above to find the interval of an eleventh, starting with one on C3. Another method is to subtract seven from eleven, which gives four. A fourth above bass clef C is F, so a fourteenth would be the F an octave above, or F4.

Primary and Secondary Triads of a Major Key

In the Western common practice period, triads are built on every scale degree of a key tonality, termed primary and secondary triads. Both primary and secondary triads contain the same accidentals that are in the key and are labeled with Roman numerals. Primary triads are more important in their harmonic function, whereas secondary triads serve as support harmonies to the primary triads. The primary triads are built on the first, fourth, and fifth scale degrees to make the tonic, subdominant, and dominant chords. In a major key, they are all major: I, IV, and V. The secondary triads are built on the second, third, sixth, and seventh scale degrees to make the supertonic, mediant, and submediant. In a major key, the supertonic, mediant, and submediant are minor, whereas the leading tone is diminished: ii, iii, vi, and vii°.

Primary and Secondary Triads of a Minor Key

In the Western common practice period, triads are built on every scale degree of a key tonality, termed primary and secondary triads. Both primary and secondary triads contain the same accidentals that are in the key and are labeled with Roman numerals. Primary triads are more important in their harmonic function, whereas secondary triads serve as support harmonies to the primary triads. The triads of a minor key commonly use the harmonic minor in which the seventh scale degree is raised by a semitone. The primary triads are built on the first, fourth, and fifth scale degrees to make the tonic, the subdominant, and the dominant chords. In a minor key, tonic and subdominant are minor, whereas the dominant is major: i, iv, and V. The secondary triads are built on the second, third, sixth, and seventh scale degrees to make the supertonic, mediant, and submediant. In a minor key, the supertonic is diminished, the median is augmented, the submediant is major, and the leading tone is diminished: ii°, III+, VI, and vii°.

Scale Degree Names and Roman Numerals for Each Note of a Scale

In the Western common practice period, diatonic scales are a series of notes in which each successive note has a scale degree based on its order in the scale. For example, the third scale degree would be the third note in the scale. Each scale degree has a diatonic function as well as voice-leading implications in terms of tendency tones and stepwise movement. Triads can be built on these scale degrees as well to create full harmonic function within a piece of music. The names for each scale degree are as follows in order: tonic, supertonic, mediant, subdominant, dominant, submediant, and leading tone. Each harmony based on a scale degree also has a corresponding Roman numeral I, ii, iii, and so on. The Roman numerals are uppercase to describe a major harmony and lowercase to describe a minor harmony.

Notation Used to Write Diminished, Augmented, Major, and Minor Triads in Roman Numerals

When notating chords in Roman numerals, the Roman numerals must correspond to the scale degree that the chord is built on. For example, the subdominant chord is built on the fourth scale degree, so the Roman numeral must be iv or IV. Present-day convention has it that major harmonies are represented by uppercase Roman numerals, whereas minor harmonies are represented by lowercase Roman numerals: IV is a major subdominant chord; iv is a minor subdominant chord. Diminished chords are related to minor chords in that they share the same root and third that is a minor third apart. Similarly, diminished chords share the lowercase designation of Roman numerals but add a diminished chord symbol in the upper right corner. For example, the diminished leading tone would be vii°. Augmented chords are related to major chords in that they share the same root and third that is a major third apart. Similarly, augmented chords share the uppercase designation of Roman numerals but add an augmented chord symbol. For example, the augmented mediant chord would be III+.

V7/Vi Chord in C Major

The V7/vi chord in C major is a secondary dominant chord. The vi chord in C major is the A minor chord, which is built on the sixth scale degree in C. In A minor, the dominant chord is based on the fifth scale degree in A, which would be E dominant seventh. The notes in the E dominant seventh chord are E, G#, B, and D.

V4/2 Chord in G Major

The V4/2 chord in G major is the dominant seventh chord in third inversion. In the G major scale, the dominant seventh is built on the fifth scale degree, D; the notes within D dominant seventh are D, F#, A, and C. In third inversion, the seventh note in the chord is the bass. Therefore, the chord should be written from bottom to top: C – D – F# – A.

VII°/III Chord in A Major

The vii°/iii chord in A major is a secondary leading tone chord. The iii chord in A major is the C# minor chord, which is built on the third scale degree in A. In C# minor, the leading tone chord is based on the seventh scale degree in C# harmonic minor, which is the B# diminished chord. The notes in the B# diminished chord are B#, D#, and F#.

Repetition, Sequence, and Imitation

Repetition, sequence, and imitation all refer to melodic devices used when developing a theme. All three devices manipulate the melodic theme in a certain way. Repetition takes the original theme and repeats the melody in the exact same way. The pitches remain the same as well as the relationships and intervals between the pitches. Sequence takes the original theme and repeats it but on a different starting pitch. Sequence maintains the same relationship and intervals between the pitches, but each pitch is now on a different note. Oftentimes, sequential repetition occurs an interval of a second or third higher or lower. Imitation takes the same original theme and repeats it but in a different voice, such as the tenor or bass instead of the soprano voice. Imitation can be strict imitation in which the intervallic relationships and key are kept the same or can also be a broadly general imitation in which rhythms, key, and voice are altered slightly.

Developing Melody Examples

Repetition

<u>Develop the following melody using repetition.</u>

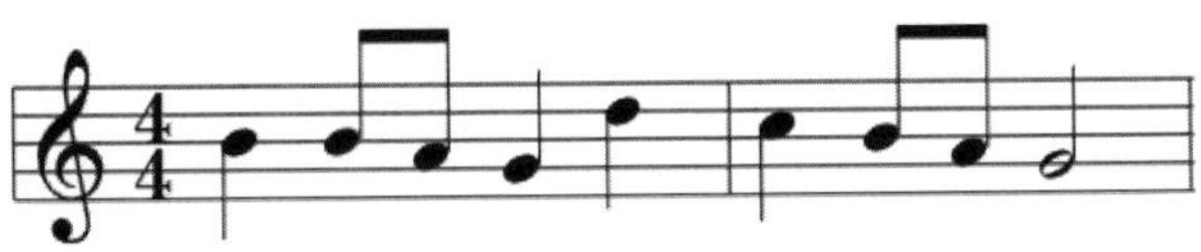

The motivic device of repetition takes an original melody and repeats it exactly on the same pitch that it originally started on. In this case, the melody that starts on B4 and repeats the exact two-bar phrase again.

Sequence

<u>Develop the Following Melody Using Sequence.</u>

The motivic device of sequence takes an original melody and repeats it but on a different note, usually on a note that is no farther than a second or third away. In this example, the original melody that starts on B4 is repeated starting on A4, a second downward. The intervallic relationships generally stay the same.

Imitation

DEVELOP THE FOLLOWING MELODY USING IMITATION.

The motivic device of imitation takes an original melody and repeats it in a different voice, usually immediately following and on the same note name. In this example, the original melody that starts on B4 in the treble clef is immediately repeated but in the bass clef on B2.

Contour in a Musical Melody

The contour of a musical line refers to the movement of the pitches, whether ascending or descending, near or far. Words that describe the contour of a melody include conjunct, which means the melody moves in a mostly stepwise manner, or disjunct, which means that the melody moves mostly in jumps farther than an interval of a second. The contour of a melody can also be terraced, which means that each successive melodic phrase starts on a pitch higher than the last. Melodies can also have an arc contour in which the pitches ascend to the middle of the melodic phrase and descend to the end. Melodies that rise and fall in a regular manner have an undulating contour, similar to the motion of a wave.

Fragmentation in Motivic Transformation

Fragmentation is a melodic device used when developing a musical theme. It occurs when a portion of the motive appears instead of the complete original idea Fragmentation can occur when the melody is repeated, but some notes are substituted with rests to create a sense of rhythmic syncopation and interest. The idea of the melody is present, but some notes have been taken out to create fragments of the original melody. Fragmentation can also occur when a portion of the original thematic material is extracted and developed separately through methods such as sequence. Instead of the entire idea of the melody being present, a small phrase is present as a reminder of the original melody and developed upon.

Fragmentation, Truncation, and Diminution in Melodies

Fragmentation, truncation, and diminution are all melodic devices used to transform a melody. All have to do with a shortening of the original thematic material, but all achieve it in different ways. Fragmentation occurs when only a part of the original motive appears; the motivic fragment tends to be developed into new material afterwards. Truncation also shortens the original motive but does not continue with new material. A truncated melody usually shortens the beginning of the original melody, unlike fragmentation, which can be any part of the original melody. Diminution also shortens a melody not by eliminating parts but by presenting the rhythms in half of its original value. For example, half notes become quarter notes when diminution occurs

Conjunct or Disjunct Examples

Example 1

Identify whether the following melody is conjunct or disjunct.

The melody in the example is disjunct. The notes move mostly by intervals larger than a second with frequent leaps.

Example 2

Identify whether the following melody is conjunct or disjunct.

The melody in the example is conjunct. The notes move primarily by step in intervals no larger than a second.

Extension and Internal Expansion of a Motive

Both extension and internal expansion refer to two melodic devices that lengthen a thematic motive. Extensions generally refer to external extensions where melodic material is added to either the beginning or the ending of a motive. When the extension adds to the beginning of the motive, it is oftentimes accompanimental in nature, helping to introduce the thematic material. When the extension adds to the end of a motive, it generally reinforces the closure of the cadence, the harmonic movement, or the melodic movement. Internal expansion refers to additional melodic material that is added within the original theme or motive. Internal expansions commonly utilize elements of repetition, sequence, and augmentation to add length within a motive.

Melodic and Rhythmic Transformation

Melodic and rhythmic transformations occur when a musical work develops a theme or motive by changing musical aspects of the original theme or motive. Melodic transformation refers to the direct change of pitches in the original theme or motive so that the melody generally becomes a different yet still similar pattern of pitches. Rhythmic transformation refers to the change of note values in the original theme or motive so that the pitches remain the same, but the pattern of each note's rhythmic value changes. Melodic transformations include devices such as repetition, sequence, imitation, fragmentation, extension, retrograde, inversion, and truncation. Rhythmic transformations include devices such as adding syncopations, dotted rhythms, rests, augmentation, diminution, and lengthening of particular notes.

Melodic Transposition

Melodic transposition is a motivic device used to develop a theme or motive by placing the theme or motive in a different key. Intervallic relationships are kept the same, as opposed to sequence, which does not keep the intervals intact but maintains the overall key of the original theme or motive. This type of melodic transposition is also called chromatic transposition because all the tonal and intervallic relationships stay the same in the new key. Diatonic transposition refers to changes such as sequence where the intervallic relationships change to maintain the original scale tones of the first theme. For example, for a motive that has the pitches D – E – F, a melodic transposition to the key of E minor would make it E – F# – G, and not E – F – G to maintain the whole step that occurs between the first two pitches in the original motive.

Example 1

Notate the transposition of the following melody into F major.

Melodic transposition generally refers to chromatic transposition where the intervallic relationships between all the notes are maintained and moved to the new key center. The original melody is in D major and starts on the tonic, moving up through the second, third, and fifth scale degrees before stepping all the way back down to tonic. To transpose this in F major, the melody should start on the tonic, F, move up through the second, third, and fifth scale degrees (G, A, and C) before stepping all the way back down through Bb, A, and G to tonic F.

Example 2

Notate the transposition of the following melody into Ab minor.

Melodic transposition generally refers to chromatic transposition where the intervallic relationships between all the notes are maintained and moved to the new key center. The original melody is in C minor, starts on the tonic, moves down and back up a fourth, and steps down through the seventh, sixth, fifth, and fourth scale degrees before moving back up a third, down a second, and down a fifth to tonic. To transpose this in Ab minor, the notes, then, should follow the same intervallic movements so that the notation starts on Ab, down to Eb, and back up to Ab, where it moves down Gb, Fb, Eb, and Db, back up a third to Fb, down a second to Eb, and finally finishing on Ab, the tonic.

Basic Compositional Skills

Conventional Parts of Four-Part Harmony

In four-part harmony, the conventional parts from high to low are soprano, alto, tenor, and bass. The general vocal range of the soprano voice is from C', middle C, to A''. The general vocal range of the alto voice is from F to D''. The general vocal range of the tenor voice is from B to G'. The general vocal range of the bass clef is from E to C'. Other vocal parts include the baritone and the mezzo-soprano; the general vocal range of the baritone is from G to E', and the general range of the mezzo-soprano is from A to F''. Although many composers use these ranges in writing a piece of four-part harmony, the voice as an instrument remains one of the most complex of instruments as each individual's voice can vary drastically in range and ability.

Close Position in Four-Part Harmony

Four-part harmony describes the style of musical composition in which there are four distinct lines of music such as that of the choral style. The four parts are known as the soprano for the top line, the alto for the lower treble line, the bass for the lowest line, and the tenor for the line just above the bass. The conventional notation for four-part writing has the stems of the soprano and tenor lines going up and the stems of the alto and bass lines going down. Close position describes four-part harmony in which no chord tones can be placed between the soprano and also lines and the alto and tenor lines; the notes are closer together than in open position.

Open Position in Four-Part Harmony

Four-part harmony describes the style of musical composition in which there are four distinct lines of music such as that of the choral style. The four parts are known as the soprano for the top line, the alto for the lower treble line, the bass for the lowest line, and the tenor for the line just above the bass. The conventional notation for four-part writing has the stems of the soprano and tenor lines going up and the stems of the alto and bass lines going down. Open position describes four-part harmony in which chord tones could be placed between the soprano and also lines and the alto and tenor lines; the notes are further away from each other than in close position, but the bass should not be more than two octaves away from the tenor.

Example 1

COMPLETE THE SOPRANO LINE IN THE FOLLOWING FOUR-PART HARMONY EXAMPLE.

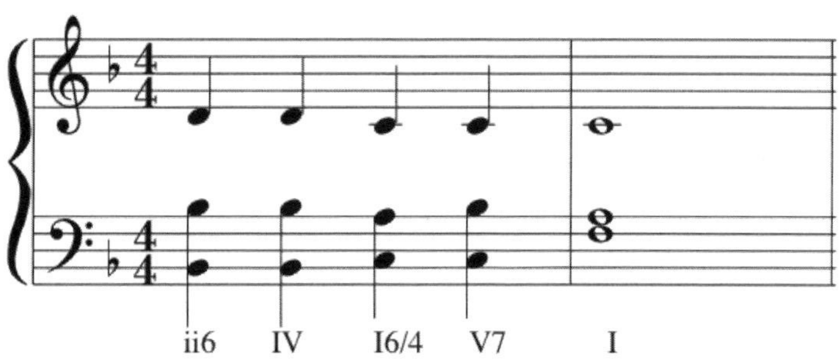

In the example, the ii6 chord in F major is the G minor chord in first inversion. Because there is no G present in the other voices, G must go in the soprano voice. Next, the IV chord, B major, does not have the fifth of the chord, so the next soprano note is F. The I6/4 chord needs the root of the I chord, which is F, and the V7 chord needs the third of the C chord, which is the E. Finally, the I chord should have the root doubled to make the soprano line as follows: G – F – F – E – F.

Example 2

COMPLETE THE TENOR LINE IN THE FOLLOWING FOUR-PART HARMONY EXAMPLE.

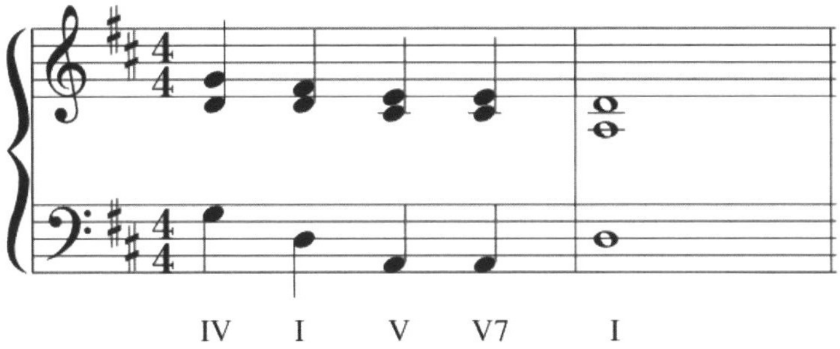

In the example, the IV chord of D major is G major. The missing note is the third, so B must go in the tenor voice. The next chord, I, which is D major, is missing the fifth, so the next tenor note is A. In the next V chord, all notes of the triad are present, so the rules of doubling have the root doubled, or A, for the next tenor note. The V7, A7, needs the seventh of the chord, so the next tenor note is G. Finally, the I chord needs the third of the chord, or F#, to make the tenor line as follows: B – A – A – G – F#.

Example 3

Complete the alto line in the following four-part harmony example.

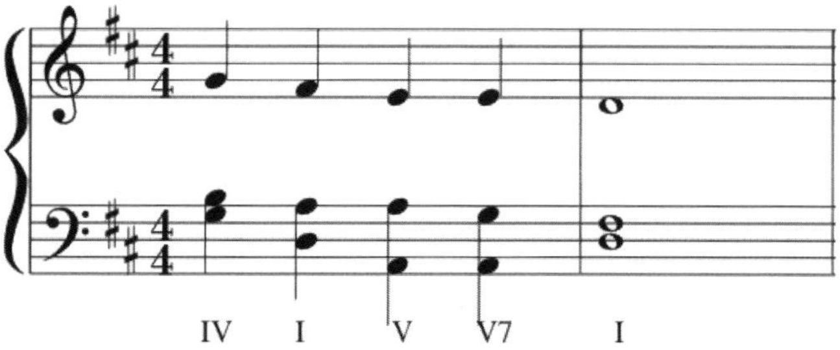

In the example, the IV chord in D major is G major; it's missing the fifth of the chord, so the D should go in the alto line. In the next chord, I (D major), all voices are present, so that root should be doubled. The V chord, or A major, is missing the third of the chord, so the C# should go in the alto line. The next V7 chord is also missing the third, so the alto should repeat the C#. Finally, the I chord is missing the fifth of the chord, which is A in the D major chord; the alto line then should be as follows: D – D – C# – C# – A.

Four-Part Writing

Doubling the Root of a Chord in Four-Part Writing

In four-part harmony, the most common chord used is the triad, which only has three notes; to create the four parts necessary for four-part writing, one of the notes will need to be doubled. Careful guidelines should be followed for the doubling of notes in the common practice style. The leading tone should never be doubled. For chords in root position, doubling the root is usually the ideal step to take for doubling. Exceptions include the diminished triad in which the third should be doubled and the V-VI progression in minor keys for which the third of the VI should be doubled. The root should also be doubled when writing first inversion triads and incomplete seventh chords.

Doubling the Third of a Chord in Four-Part Writing

In four-part harmony, the most common chord used is the triad, which has only three notes; to create the four parts necessary for four-part writing, one of the notes will need to be doubled. Careful guidelines should be followed for the doubling of notes in the common practice style. The leading tone should never be doubled. For diminished triads, the third should always be doubled so that any tone of the tritone is not doubled. In minor keys, the VI of the V-VI progression should have the third doubled. Doubling the third in first inversion minor chords is also acceptable. The third should not be doubled in second inversion chords or dominant seventh chords.

Doubling the Fifth of a Chord in Four-Part Writing

In four-part harmony, the most common chord used is the triad, which only has three notes; to create the four parts necessary for four-part writing, one of the notes will need to be doubled. Careful guidelines should be followed for the doubling of notes in the common practice style. The leading tone should never be doubled. When writing second inversion chords, the bass note, or the fifth, should always be doubled; the root and third of a second inversion chord should never be doubled. In first inversion chords of the tonic, subdominant, and dominant, the fifth may also be doubled. The fifth should not be doubled in a submediant chord. The fifth can also be doubled in a dominant chord.

Writing Seventh Chords in Four-Part Writing

When writing seventh chords in four-part writing, careful guidelines should be followed to avoid doubling the leading tone. In a dominant seventh chord, the third of the chord is the leading tone and thus should never be doubled. Because these chords have four pitches, all four notes of the dominant seventh chord may be used, or the fifth of the chord may be left out. If writing an incomplete seventh chord, the root should be doubled while including the third and the seventh of the chord. The seventh note should also not be doubled. The third of the chord should not be left out because it gives each chord its quality of major or minor.

Example 1

WRITE THE II6/4 CHORD IN BB MAJOR IN FOUR VOICES WITH APPROPRIATE DOUBLING AND EXPLAIN.

The ii6/4 chord in Bb major is a C minor chord in second inversion. The notes in this chord are C – Eb – G. Because it is in second inversion, G should be the bass note. The appropriate doubling for chords in second inversion has the fifth note being doubled; the root and the third should not be doubled. In four-part harmony, this chord should be, from bass to soprano voices, G, C, Eb, and G.

Example 2

WRITE THE VI CHORD IN G MAJOR IN FOUR VOICES WITH APPROPRIATE DOUBLING AND EXPLAIN.

The vi chord in G major is an E minor chord in root position. The notes in this chord are E – G – B. Because this chord is in root position, E should be the bass note. Generally, the ideal doubling for the vi chord in root position has the third of the chord doubled; however, the root can also be doubled. In four-part harmony, this chord should be spelled, from bass to soprano voices, E, G, G, and B.

Example 3

Write the I6 chord in Eb major in four voices with appropriate doubling and explain.

The I6 chord in Eb major is an Eb major chord in first inversion. The notes in this chord are Eb – G – Bb. Because this chord is in first inversion, the bass note should be G. The appropriate doubling for I6 chords is to double the root in the soprano voice. The fifth may also be doubled but never the third of the chord. In four-part harmony, the chord can be spelled, from bass to soprano voices, G, Bb, Eb, and Bb.

Example 4

WRITE THE V6 CHORD IN A MAJOR IN FOUR VOICES WITH APPROPRIATE DOUBLING AND EXPLAIN.

The V6 chord in A major is an E major chord in first inversion. The notes in this chord are E – G# – B. Because this chord is in first inversion, the bass note should be G#. The appropriate doubling for V6 chords is to double the root or the fifth note; the third of the chord should not be doubled. In four-part harmony, the chord can be spelled, from bass to soprano voices, G#, E, B, and E.

Example 5

WRITE THE II6 CHORD IN E MAJOR IN FOUR VOICES WITH APPROPRIATE DOUBLING AND EXPLAIN.

The ii6 chord in E major is an F# minor chord in first inversion. The notes in this chord are F# – A – C#. Because this chord is in first inversion, the bass note should be A. The appropriate doubling for ii6 chords is to double the third of the chord. The root can also be doubled, but the fifth should not be doubled. In four-part harmony, the chord can be spelled, from bass to soprano voices, A, C#, F#, and A.

Example 6

WRITE THE III6 CHORD IN AB MAJOR IN FOUR VOICES WITH APPROPRIATE DOUBLING AND EXPLAIN.

The iii6 chord in Ab major is a C minor chord in first inversion. The notes in this chord are C – Eb – G. Because this chord is in first inversion, the bass note should be Eb. The appropriate doubling for iii6 chords is to double the third note of the chord. The root can also be doubled, but the fifth should not be doubled. In four-part harmony, the chord can be spelled, from bass to soprano voices, Eb, C, G, and Eb.

Example 7

WRITE THE V/V CHORD IN D MAJOR IN FOUR VOICES WITH APPROPRIATE DOUBLING AND EXPLAIN.

The V/V chord in D major is a secondary dominant chord; the dominant of the dominant in D major, which is A major, is an E major chord. The notes in this chord are E – G# B. The appropriate doubling for secondary dominants is to double the root of the chord. The altered note, G# in this case, should never be doubled. In four-part harmony, the chord can be spelled, from bass to soprano voices, E, B, G#, and E.

Example 8

WRITE THE III+ CHORD IN B MINOR IN FOUR VOICES WITH APPROPRIATE DOUBLING AND EXPLAIN.

The III+ chord in B minor is the augmented D chord in root position. The notes in this chord are D – F# – A#. The appropriate doubling for augmented chords is for the third of the chord to be doubled. The root can also be doubled, but the altered note, A# in this case, should never be doubled. In four-part harmony, the chord can be spelled, from bass to soprano voices, D, A#, F#, and D.

Example 9

WRITE THE V/III CHORD IN G MAJOR IN FOUR VOICES WITH APPROPRIATE DOUBLING AND EXPLAIN.

The V/iii chord in G major is a secondary dominant chord; the dominant of the mediant in G major, which is B minor, is the F# major chord. The notes in this chord are F# – A# – C#. The appropriate doubling for secondary dominants is to double the root of the chord. The altered notes, A# and C# in this case, should never be doubled. In four-part harmony, the chord can be spelled, from bass to soprano voices, F#, A#, C#, and F#.

TENDENCY TONES

Much of the rules and guidelines in four-part harmony concern the movement and resolutions of tendency tones. Tendency tones are highly unstable notes within a chord that demand to be resolved to its closest stable pitch. This hierarchy is usually described in terms of scale degree numbers. The resolution of tendency tones can either be half steps or whole steps, but they are usually resolved in a downward and stepwise motion. The strongest tendency tone is the leading tone, which should be resolved by an upward half-step motion. Other tendency tones include scale degree six to five, scale degree four to three, and scale degree two to one. Altered scale degrees through sharps or flats also resolve toward the closest stable scale degree. For example, a flat sixth scale degree would resolve to the fifth scale degree.

Function of the Tonic, Predominant, and Dominant in Typical Harmonic Progressions

In a harmonic progression of the common practice period, chords typically have one of three harmonic functions: tonic, predominant, and dominant. The tonic function serves as the strongest chord that defines the key of a piece of music. It is the sense of home and resolution in the music and usually the end goal of the harmonic progression. The dominant function serves as the function that expresses the most harmonic tension. It gives the music a sense of unease and motion; the tendency is strongest for the dominant function to want to resolve to tonic. The predominant function serves as the move away from the foundational tonic and as a preparation for dominant chords. Predominant function creates variety and interest in the moments between tonic and dominant functions.

Relationship of Fifths in Harmonic Progression

Harmonic progression refers to the movement of chords from one to the next that provides for a smooth transition between specific tendency tones in each chord. There are many progressions that provide for smooth harmonic movement, and one common one utilizes the relationship of fifths in its progression. In it, a dominant chord resolves to a tonic chord that becomes the dominant chord to the next tonic. This progresses until the music reaches the original tonic at the end. This relationship works well in major keys as well as minor keys. Other relationships include the mediant to the submediant, the submediant to the supertonic, the tonic to the subdominant, and the supertonic to the dominant; all involve the cyclic relationship of fifths in progressions.

Chord Substitutions for the I, V, and IV Chords

The I, V, and IV each serve a specific harmonic function. Any chords that are used to substitute the I, V, and IV chords must also contribute to that overall harmonic function. The I chord is the tonic and also serves the tonic function as the strongest chord that defines the key of a piece of music. Other chords that can be substituted while still maintaining the tonic foundation of the key are the mediant iii chord and the submediant chord. The V chord is the dominant and serves the dominant function that expresses harmonic tension. Other chords that can be used are leading tone and the dominant seventh chords. The IV chord is the subdominant and serves the predominant function that expresses a move away from the foundation and a preparation for dominant chords. Other chords that can be used are the supertonic and submediant chords.

Role of the Soprano, Alto, Tenor, and Bass Lines in Good Voice Leading

When creating four-part harmony in the style of the Baroque practice, the four lines should be thought of as the soprano, alto, tenor, and bass lines of the piece. The soprano line can be described as the melody and should contain mostly conjunct, stepwise movements with perhaps a few leaps to maintain interest and variety. The alto and tenor voices act as harmonic support and also aid in the movements of the soprano and bass lines; the alto and tenor lines should be relatively stable in their movements without too many leaps. The bass line provides the harmony of each chord, and contains more leaps than the alto and tenor lines, but should also not have excessive jumps or leaps that create unacceptable movements, such as objectionable parallels.

Voice Leading

Voice leading in four-part harmony creates opportunities for smooth and conjunct movement of the voices. The common tone is an important aspect of voice-leading decisions and helps to maintain a pleasing and logical progression of voices. The common tone refers to a pitch that is shared from one chord to the next in four-part harmony. The common tone should usually be maintained when moving from one chord to the next because it aids in the smooth transition of the other voices in a stepwise manner. If the common tone is ignored and jumps for example from the tenor voice to the soprano voice, this creates a disjunct sound with poor voice leading. Common tones tend to be approached by step and left by step.

When writing a musical composition in four-part harmony, one must make certain that the voice leading within the music leads to a smooth and pleasing sound. Voices should move in a clean and mostly stepwise motion to facilitate ease of singing. Poor voice leading leads to a choppy and unpleasing sound that is often disjunct and difficult to sing. Good voice leading resolves tendency tones to their most logical pitch, whereas poor voice leading does not resolve tendency tones. Good voice leading avoids intervals of the fifth and octave in parallel motion, but intervals of parallel sixths and thirds are acceptable and encouraged. Good voice leading utilizes occasional leaps to create variety and interest, whereas poor voice leading creates too many leaps that create awkward and unpleasant sounds within the music.

Two Voices Moving in Parallel Motion

In four-part harmony, there are many types of movements between voices, including parallel motion. Parallel motion has both acceptable and unacceptable conditions for movement of voices. Acceptable conditions for parallel motion are movements in intervals of thirds and sixths. Two voices must move in the same direction with the same intervallic relationship of thirds or sixths. Unacceptable conditions for parallel motion are movements in the intervals of fifths and octaves. If two voices move in the same direction with the same intervallic relationship, care must be taken for them not to move in intervals of fifths or octaves as this creates objectionable parallels. Voices moving in the interval of parallel fourths are only acceptable if another two voices move in parallel thirds at the same time to support the movement.

Similar, Contrary, Oblique, and Parallel Motions

When writing a musical composition in four-part harmony, there are many types of movements between voices. Similar motion refers to voices that move in the same direction but not necessarily the same intervallic relationships. For example, two voices move upward, but one moves up a third, while the other one moves up a sixth. Contrary motion refers to voices that move in opposite directions. Oblique motion refers to voice movement where one voices stays the same and the other voice moves. For example, one voice stays on C, while the other voice moves from G to B. Parallel motion refers to voices that move in the same direction and also with the same intervallic relationships such as in third, sixths, or seconds.

Voice Crossing, Direct Fifths, Direct Octaves, and Voice Exchange

Voice crossing, direct fifths, direct octaves, and voice exchange all refer to types of movement within four-part harmony. Voice crossing refers to the movement of voices when two voices exchange positions. For example, the soprano note moves below the alto voice in a crossed voice manner. Although acceptable, this type of movement should only be used occasionally. Direct fifths refers to the interval of a fifth between two voices that is approached by similar motion. Direct octaves refer to the interval of an octave between two voices that is approached by similar motion. Other names for these movements are hidden fifths and hidden octaves; these movements in four-part harmony are to be avoided. Voice exchange refers to the trading of notes between two different voices. For example, tenor and bass play E to G and G to E, respectively.

Poor Voice Leading

When writing a musical composition in four-part harmony, there are many types of poor voice leading that should absolutely be avoided. Voices should never move in certain parallel motion such as parallel fifths or parallel octaves. These intervals are known as objectionable parallels and should be avoided at all costs. Parallel fourths are only acceptable with the presence of a parallel third to support the movement. Voices should never overlap; a higher voice should never move lower than the next lower note and vice versa when moving in similar motion. There should never be chromatic movement from a soprano voice to the next bass note. Leading tones should always be resolved by moving up a half step to the tonic. If a leading tone is part of a secondary dominant chord, it should be resolved by moving down a half step.

Example 1

IDENTIFY THE PROBLEM IN THE FOLLOWING EXAMPLE OF POOR VOICE LEADING.

The musical example contains poor voice leading of parallel fifths in the alto and soprano voices. The F and C should not move to G and D in the alto and soprano lines, respectively, to avoid the case of parallel fifths.

Example 2

IDENTIFY THE PROBLEM IN THE FOLLOWING EXAMPLE OF POOR VOICE LEADING.

The musical example contains poor voice leading of an unresolved leading tone. The leading tone of the first dominant chord—B—should lead to the tonic note C. In this case, it jumps down to the fifth scale degree, which is unacceptable for proper voice leading.

Example 3

IDENTIFY THE PROBLEM IN THE FOLLOWING EXAMPLE OF POOR VOICE LEADING.

The musical example contains poor voice leading of overlapping voices in the alto and soprano lines. The first alto voice of C4 moves to F4 in the next chord, which is higher than the first soprano voice of Eb4. The voices should not move to a note higher than the note of the previous upper voice.

Example 4

IDENTIFY THE PROBLEM IN THE FOLLOWING EXAMPLE OF POOR VOICE LEADING.

The musical example contains poor voice leading of cross or false relations. The soprano voice of the first chord creates a tritone relationship with the bass note of the second chord—the interval of an augmented fourth from Bb to E—and should be avoided.

Example 5

IDENTIFY THE PROBLEM IN THE FOLLOWING EXAMPLE OF POOR VOICE LEADING.

The musical example contains poor voice leading of parallel octaves. The bass line and soprano lines create objectionable parallel voices in the movement from G to A. The soprano line should move from G down to E to avoid the parallel motion.

Example 6

IDENTIFY THE PROBLEM IN THE FOLLOWING EXAMPLE OF POOR VOICE LEADING.

The musical example contains poor voice leading of parallel fourths. The alto and soprano lines should not move from E to F# and A to B, respectively, to avoid the poor voice leading of parallel fourths because they are not supported by the simultaneous movement of parallel thirds.

BASS NOTES INDICATED BY THE 5/3, 6/3, AND 6/4 CHORD SYMBOLS

The 5/3, 6/3, and 6/4 chord symbols all refer to the figured bass of a triad. Figured bass refers to the common practice during the Baroque era in which composers wrote a bass line with symbols for what specific harmonies were to be played. The figured bass symbol 5/3 refers to a triad in root position; the 6/3 figured bass symbol refers to a triad in first inversion; and the 6/4 figured bass symbol refers to a triad in second inversion. A triad in root position will have the root note as the bass note. A triad in first inversion will have the third tone as the bass note. A triad in second inversion will have the fifth note as the bass note.

BASS NOTES INDICATED BY THE 7, 6/5, 4/3, AND 4/2 CHORD SYMBOLS

The 7, 6/5, 4/3, and 4/2 chord symbols all refer to the figured bass of a seventh chord. Figured bass refers to the common practice during the Baroque era in which composers wrote a bass line with symbols for what specific harmonies were to be played. The figured bass symbol 7 indicates root position; 6/5 indicates first inversion; 4/3 indicates second inversion, and 4/2 indicates third inversion. In root position, the bass note will be the root of the seventh chord. In first inversion, the bass note will be the third note of the seventh chord. In second inversion, the bass note will be the fifth note of the seventh chord. In third inversion, the bass note will be the seventh note of the seventh chord.

Chord Alterations Indicated by the Sharp, Flat, Natural, Slash, and Plus Symbols

The sharp, flat, natural, slash, and plus symbols all refer to modifications or alterations to a given note in a chord. A sharp symbol, notated by the symbol ♯, indicates for that note to be raised by a half step. For example, D major ♯5 would have the fifth note raised by a half step. A flat symbol, notated by the symbol ♭, indicates for that note to be lowered by a half step. For example, D major ♭5 would have the fifth note lowered by a half step. A natural symbol, notated by the symbol ♮, indicates for any alterations on the note to be canceled and to play the natural note. A slash symbol, notated by the symbol \ or + indicates for that note to be raised by a half step. For example, D major 3+ would have the third note raised by a half step.

Writing Bass Line Examples

Example 1

Write the bass line that should be added to the following melody.

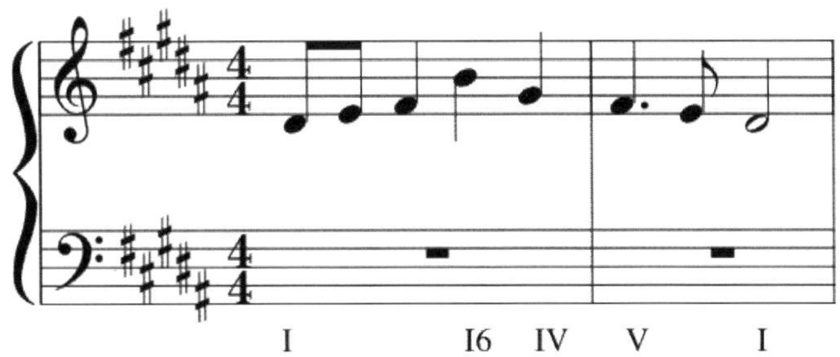

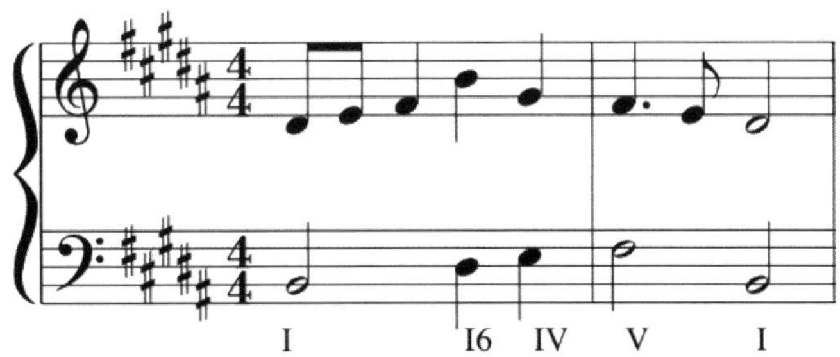

In the example, the first chord is the I chord, which is B major. The first bass note then should be B. The next chord is I6, which is B major in first inversion; the next bass note should be D#. The root of the IV chord is E of E major. The root of the V chord is F# of the F# major triad, and finally, the last I chord should have the bass note of B, which is the root of the B major chord.

Example 2

WRITE THE BASS LINE THAT SHOULD BE ADDED TO THE FOLLOWING MELODY.

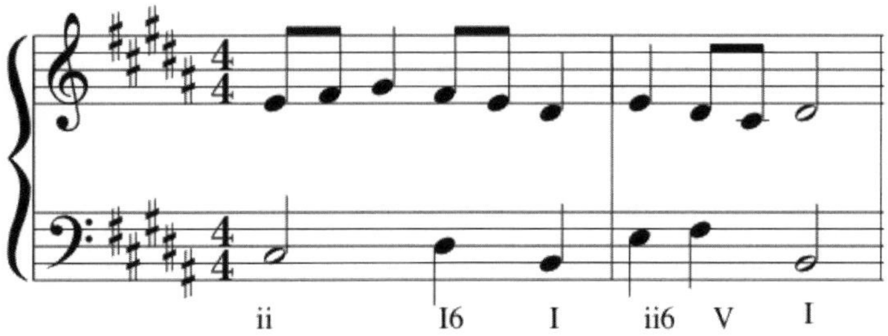

In the example, the first chord is a ii chord in root position; the bass note should be C# of the C# minor chord. The next chord is I6, which is B major in first inversion. This means that the bass note should be the third of the chord, or D#. The next chord is the I chord, which has B as the next bass note. The ii6 chord is C# in first inversion, which means that the bass note should be E. The V chord is F# major, and the I chord is B major, so the last two bass notes are F# and B.

SIMILARITIES AND DIFFERENCE BETWEEN FIGURED BASS AND LEAD SHEETS FOR MUSICAL PERFORMANCE

Figured bass refers to the common practice during the Baroque era in which composers wrote a bass line with symbols for what specific harmonies were to be played; the exact notes to be played for the keyboard or continuo were not provided. Musicians at the time were adept at realizing the figured bass and improvising music based solely on a bass line and corresponding harmonies. Lead sheets refer to the present-day practice of notation in which a melody is provided with corresponding chord symbols but without the music written out, similarly to figured bass. Both require musicians to improvise over the given chords. In figured bass, the chords are represented by Roman numerals for their respective scale degree and function within the music, whereas on lead sheets, they are typically notated by the actual chord names, for example, Em, G, Adim.

Score Analysis

Imperfect and Perfect Cadences

The terms *imperfect* and *perfect* cadences apply to the authentic and plagal cadences. An authentic or plagal cadence classifies as perfect if both of the chords are in root position and the tonic pitch sounds in the highest voice. An authentic or plagal cadence classifies as imperfect if either of the chords are in an inversion and/or the tonic pitch does not sound in the highest voice. An example of a perfect authentic cadence is the progression V to I with the tonic of the last chord sounding in the highest voice. An example of an imperfect authentic cadence is the progression V^6 to I. An example of a perfect plagal cadence is the progression IV to I with the tonic of the last chord sounding in the highest voice. An example of an imperfect plagal cadence is the IV-to-I progression in which the last chord does not contain the tonic in the highest-sounding voice.

Deceptive Cadence

A cadence is a combination of chords that make up a closing or ending of a musical section, phrase, or movement. Cadences mark a harmonic, melodic, and rhythmic arrival point in the music. A deceptive cadence is defined as any cadence that usually moves from a dominant V to tonic I and moves to the submediant vi instead. Aurally, the effect is that of surprise as the expectation when hearing the dominant V is for the dominant to resolve to the tonic chord; instead, the cadence deceives the ear, thus the name *deceptive cadence*. Less commonly, the deceptive cadence consists of a subdominant IV moving to the submediant vi chord or a dominant V chord moving to a *b*VI chord. Deceptive cadences are considered to be inconclusive.

Plagal Cadence

A cadence is a combination of chords that make up a closing or ending of a musical section, phrase, or movement. Cadences mark a harmonic, melodic, and rhythmic arrival point in the music. Plagal cadences are defined as any cadence that progresses from the subdominant IV chord to the tonic I chord. The plagal cadence is also known as the church cadence or the amen cadence from its popularity in the sixteenth century. The plagal cadence does not sound as finite as the authentic cadence because the subdominant IV chord lacks the leading tone, which has a strong tendency to move to the tonic. Instead, both the fourth and sixth scale degrees resolve to the third and fifth scale degrees, respectively, in creating a finished, conclusive cadence.

Cadence Examples

Example 1

Write a V6-I Authentic cadence in F# major on the bass clef and explain.

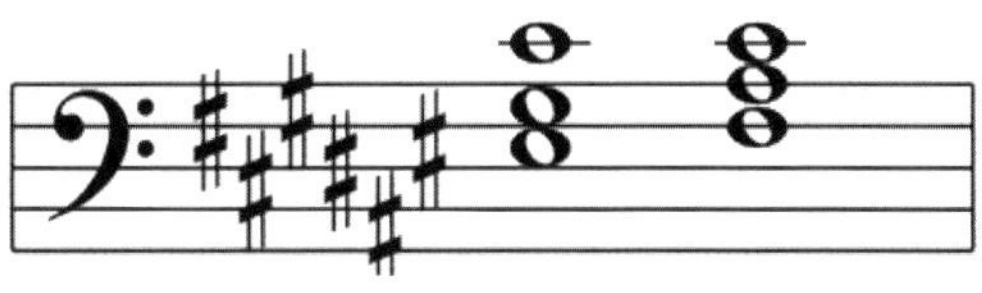

In F# major, the V6 chord is the dominant chord based on the fifth scale degree: C# major. The 6 indicates first inversion, which would have E# as the bass note. In an authentic cadence, the I chord should be in root position so that the voice leading from E# in the bass moves upward by step to F#.

Example 2

WRITE A IV6-V PHRYGIAN HALF CADENCE IN B MINOR ON THE BASS CLEF AND EXPLAIN.

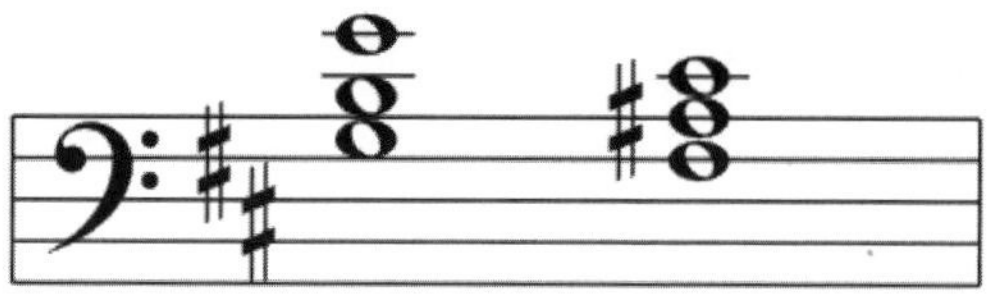

In B minor, the iv6 chord is the subdominant chord in first inversion, that is, E minor with G in the bass. Because this chord is moving to the dominant F# chord in B major, all voices should move downward to resolve all tendency tones.

Example 3

WRITE AN IV6-I6/4 PLAGAL CADENCE IN D MAJOR ON THE TREBLE CLEF AND EXPLAIN.

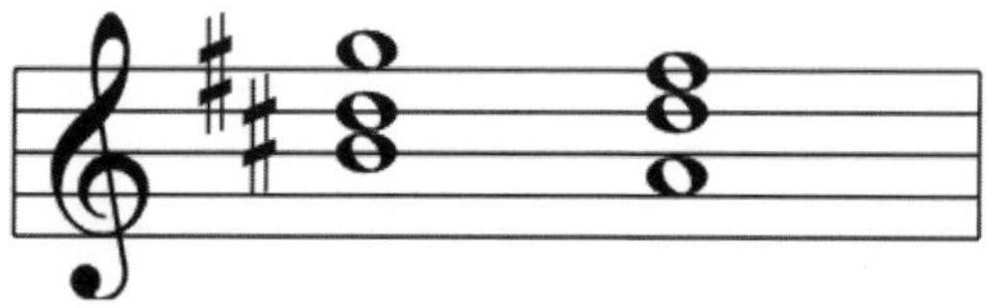

In D major, the IV6 chord is the subdominant chord in first inversion: G major with B as the bass note. The I6/4 chord is the tonic chord in second inversion: D major with A in the bass. Because D is a common tone, it should stay in the same voice, while the other voices move downward.

Example 4

WRITE AN IV-VI6/4 DECEPTIVE CADENCE IN F# MINOR ON THE BASS CLEF AND EXPLAIN.

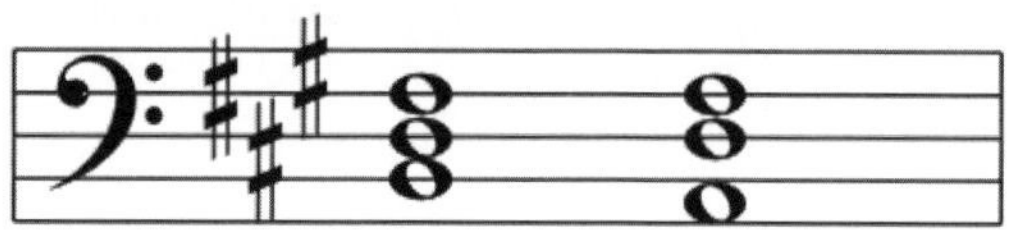

In F# minor, the iv chord is the subdominant chord in root position: B minor with B as the bass note. The VI6/4 chord indicates the submediant chord in second inversion: D major with A as the bass note. Because both the D and F# are common tones in both chords, only the bass voice should move downward from B to A.

Example 5

WRITE A V6/V-V HALF CADENCE IN DB MAJOR ON THE TREBLE CLEF AND EXPLAIN.

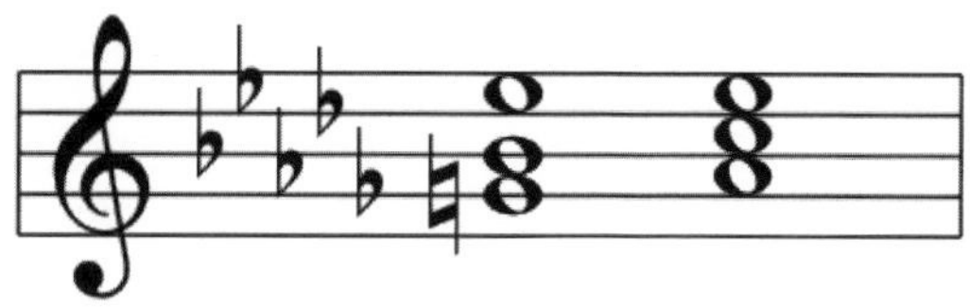

In Db major, the V6/V chord is the secondary dominant in first inversion or the dominant of the dominant: Eb major with G as the bass note. The V chord is the dominant chord in root position: Ab major with Ab as the bass note. Eb is the common tone between both chords and should stay in the same voice. The other voices should move upward in resolving the tendency tones.

Suspension, Escape Tone, and Passing Tone

A nonharmonic tone is not contained in a certain harmony. Other names for nonharmonic tones are *embellishing tones* and *non-chord tones*. A suspension describes a nonharmonic tone in which a tone from one chord is held over to another chord, creating a dissonance. The dissonant tone is then resolved by stepping downward. Common suspensions are the 4-3 suspension, 9-8 suspension, and the 7-6 suspension. An escape tone describes a non-chord tone on a weak beat that is approached by an upward step from a chord tone and resolved by a leap in the opposite direction. A passing tone describes a non-chord tone on a weak beat that is approached by step and resolved by another step in the same direction.

Anticipation, Retardation, and a Neighbor Nonharmonic Tone

A nonharmonic tone is not contained in a certain harmony. Other names for nonharmonic tones are embellishing tones and non-chord tones. An anticipation tone describes a dissonant note that appears before becoming a consonant note in the harmony in which it is contained. It occurs on a weak beat, is approached by a step, and is resolved by repeating the same note. A retardation note describes a non-chord tone on a strong beat that is approached by the same pitch and resolved by a step up. A neighbor note describes a non-chord tone on a weak beat that is approached by a step either above or below and resolved by step back to the approach tone. Another name for a neighbor tone is an *auxiliary tone*.

Nonharmonic Neighbor Tones as Opposed to Neighbor Groups

Nonharmonic tones are not contained within a certain harmony. Other names for nonharmonic tones are *embellishing tones* and non-chord tones. A neighbor tone describes a non-chord tone on a weak beat that is approached by a step either above or below and resolved by step back to the approach tone. Another name for a neighbor tone is an *auxiliary tone*. A neighbor group is similar to an escape tone, except that in neighbor groups, a non-chord tone on a weak beat is approached by a skip from a chord tone and resolved by a step in the opposite direction while maintaining similar motion to the other voices. Other names for neighbor groups are *changing tones* and *changing notes*.

Trill, Mordent, Turn, Appoggiatura, and Grace Note

Trills, mordents, turns, appoggiaturas, and grace notes, all describe a specific type of nonharmonic tone called *ornaments* or *embellishments*. Ornaments are tones that are not contained within a certain harmony, and are usually indicated by symbols, but can also be written out. A trill is performed by quickly alternating between the written note and a neighbor note. A mordent is performed by playing the written note, the note below it, and then returning to the written note. Playing the note above the written note, the written note, the note below it, and then returning to the written note perform a turn. An appoggiatura is performed by playing the note above the written note on the beat and then playing the main note. A grace note is performed by playing the note above the written note before the beat and then playing the main note.

Pedal Point and an Ostinato

Both the pedal point and the ostinato are nonharmonic tones found in the bass voice that are sometimes not contained within a certain harmony and are dissonant. A pedal point is usually a sustained tone in the bass voice for an extended amount of time. Unlike other nonharmonic tones, pedal points usually start as a consonant note that when held, become dissonant with the moving parts until it is resolved back to a consonant note with the other voices. An ostinato is repeated pattern that is constant in the bass voice that can also become dissonant as the upper voices move. An ostinato is usually a motif or phrase that is repeated in the same line.

Nonharmonic Tone Examples

Example 1

Identify the Following Nonharmonic Tone.

The nonharmonic tone in the example is an anticipation tone. The D of the second chord, G minor, is played before the chord as if "anticipating" the chord. This creates a non-chord tone in the first chordal harmony.

Example 2

Identify the Following Nonharmonic Tone.

The nonharmonic tone in the example is a lower neighbor note. The B steps away on a weak beat from the C chord tone in a downward manner and steps back up to the C chord tone.

Example 3

Identify the Following Nonharmonic Tone.

The nonharmonic tone in the example is a chromatic passing tone. The Bb moves on a weak beat between two chord tones in a semitone manner like that in a chromatic scale.

Example 4

Identify the Following Nonharmonic Tone.

The nonharmonic tone in the example is an appoggiatura. The Ab is on the strong downbeat and steps downward to the G chord tone.

Example 5

IDENTIFY THE FOLLOWING NONHARMONIC TONE.

The nonharmonic tone in the example is an escape tone. The D is an upward step on a weak beat followed by a skip downward in the opposite direction to the B chord tone.

Example 6

IDENTIFY THE FOLLOWING NONHARMONIC TONE.

The nonharmonic tone in the example is a rearticulated suspension. The Ab from the first chord is restated as a nonharmonic tone on the strong beat of the second chord and introduced as a suspension that is resolved downward by step.

Example 7

IDENTIFY THE FOLLOWING NONHARMONIC TONE.

The nonharmonic tone in the example is a grace note. The grace note on E is played quickly right before the main note, D. Grace notes always have a slash through the stem.

Example 8

IDENTIFY THE FOLLOWING NONHARMONIC TONE.

The nonharmonic tone in the example is a mordent. Mordents are indicated by its symbol with a vertical line through it. The mordent should be played as the main note, D, the C a step below the main note, and a step back up to the main note, D.

Example 9

IDENTIFY THE FOLLOWING NONHARMONIC TONE.

The nonharmonic tone in the example is a trill. Trills are indicated either by the abbreviation *tr* or by the trill symbol. The trill should be played as a rapid alternation between the main note and the note above it: C and D in this case.

Example 10

IDENTIFY THE FOLLOWING NONHARMONIC TONE.

The nonharmonic tone in the example is a turn. Turns are indicated by the curved turn symbol above the note. This turn should be played as E – D – C – D.

Example 11

IDENTIFY THE FOLLOWING NONHARMONIC TONE.

The nonharmonic tone in the example is a double neighbor. The non-chord tone A is approached by step from the chord tone B, skips up to the other non-chord tone a step away from B which is C, and returns by step to the non-chord tone B.

TONICIZATION AND MODULATION

Tonicization and modulation both refer to music that has changed keys or shifted its tonic. Tonicization refers to a key change that is relatively short such as a few measures, versus modulation, in which the key changes lasts for many bars or for an entire section. In both occurrences, a new key is established through harmonic movement and cadences. Both tonicization and modulation commonly use key relationships such as closely related keys, enharmonically equivalent keys, and parallel keys. Closely related keys are often no more than one sharp or flat away from the original key. Enharmonically equivalent keys use different key signatures for the same-sounding harmonies. Parallel keys share the same tonic but differ in modality, such as major and minor. All of these key relationships aid the harmonic movement in tonicization and modulation.

PIVOT CHORD MODULATION

A pivot chord modulation, also known as a common chord modulation, aids in the modulation of a piece of music from one key to another. This type of modulation is the most common type of modulation between one key to the next. In a pivot chord modulation, both keys share a commonly spelled chord that acts in different functions in each key. The pivot chord usually appears before the first chromatic alteration of the new key that is usually a closely related key. For example, the modulation of C major to G major might include the pivot chord C major triad that is spelled the same way in C major as in G major. In C major, this triad functions as the tonic or I chord; in G major, this triad functions as the subdominant or IV chord. As the music cadences in C major from dominant to tonic, the pivot chord uses the C major triad as the new subdominant chord to move to the dominant chord.

Common Tone Modulation

A common tone modulation, also known as a pivot tone modulation, aids in the modulation of a piece of music from one key to another. In a common tone modulation, both keys share a common note at the site of modulation, but they do not share a common chord. The common tone usually appears before the first chromatic alteration of the new key that is usually a closely related key. For example, the modulation of C major to Eb major might include the common tone C in the two chords surrounding the site of modulation. In the first key of C major, the common tone C appears in the tonic chord; in the key of Eb major, the common tone C appears in the subdominant chord.

Phrase Modulation

A phrase modulation, also known as a direct modulation, aids in the modulation of a piece of music from one key to another. This type of modulation results in a more abrupt modulation as there is no shared chord or tone. A phrase modulation occurs at the end of the last phrase in the original key and the beginning of the next phrase in the new key. For example, in the modulation of C major to D major through a phrase or direct modulation, the last phrase of C major ends with a perfect authentic cadence. The next measure begins the new phrase in D major with a direct change to D major as the tonic chord without any shared chords or tones.

Modulation Examples

Example 1

Describe the Original Key, the Key the Music Modulates to, and the Type of Modulation in the Following Excerpt.

In the example, the original key is D major, as seen in the perfect authentic cadence from V to I in the first measure. The new key in the second measure is A major, also with an authentic cadence from V to I. The type of modulation used is the pivot chord modulation; the D major chord in the first measure acts as tonic in the first key of D major while simultaneously acting as the subdominant chord in A major.

Example 2

DESCRIBE THE ORIGINAL KEY, THE KEY THE MUSIC MODULATES TO, AND THE TYPE OF MODULATION IN THE FOLLOWING EXCERPT.

In the example, the original key is A major, as seen in the perfect authentic cadence from V to I in the first measure. The new key in the second measure is C major, with a plagal cadence from IV to I. The type of modulation used is the common tone modulation; both the I chord in A major and the IV chord in C major contain the common tone of A4.

Example 3

DESCRIBE THE ORIGINAL KEY, THE KEY THE MUSIC MODULATES TO, AND THE TYPE OF MODULATION IN THE FOLLOWING EXCERPT.

In the example, the original key is E major, as seen in the perfect authentic cadence from V to I in the first measure. The new key in the second measure is B major, also with an authentic cadence from V to I. The type of modulation used is the phrase modulation; the cadence in the first measure finishes the first phrase, and the music continues to the new phrase in the new key without shared tones or pivot chords.

EXAMPLES OF KEYS

Example 1

WRITE THE KEY OF E MAJOR AND EXPLAIN.

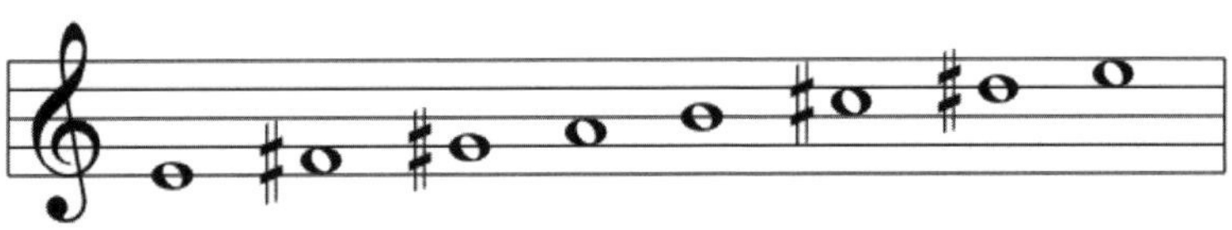

The key of E major contains a series of notes with the following pattern of half (H) and whole (W) steps: W-W-H-W-W-W-H. To find which notes require accidentals, take four turns around the circle of fifths to find E major: Four turns equals the four sharps of F#, C#, G#, and D#.

Example 2

WRITE THE KEY OF F# NATURAL MINOR AND EXPLAIN.

The key of F# natural minor contains a series of notes with the following pattern of half (H) and whole (W) steps: W-H-W-W-H-W-W. To find which notes require accidentals, take four turns around the minor circle of fifths to find F# minor: Three turns equals the three sharps of F#, C#, and G#.

Example 3

WRITE THE KEY OF C HARMONIC MINOR AND EXPLAIN.

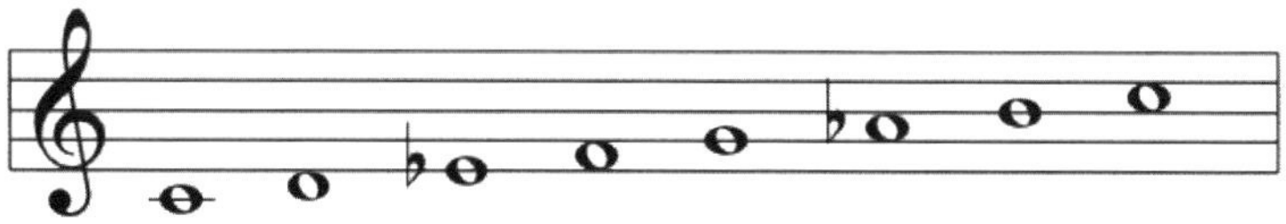

The key of C harmonic minor is the natural minor scale with a raised seventh scale degree. The key of C natural minor contains Eb, Ab, and Bb. The seventh scale degree is Bb, which becomes B natural in C harmonic minor.

Example 4

WRITE THE KEY OF A MELODIC MINOR, ASCENDING AND DESCENDING, AND EXPLAIN.

The key of A melodic minor is the natural minor scale with raised sixth and seventh scale degrees ascending and cancelled sixth and seventh alterations descending. The key of A natural minor has no accidentals. To make the melodic minor, the F and G of the sixth and seventh scale degrees become F# and G# ascending and return to their natural keys descending.

Example 5

WRITE A PENTATONIC SCALE STARTING ON C AND EXPLAIN.

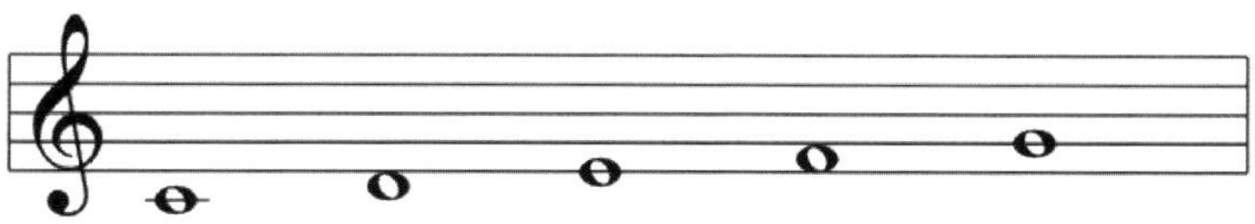

The pentatonic scale contains five notes with the most common whole (W) and half (H) step pattern: W-W-H-W. Starting on C, the notes are C, D, E, F, and G.

Example 6

WRITE A WHOLE TONE SCALE STARTING ON A AND EXPLAIN.

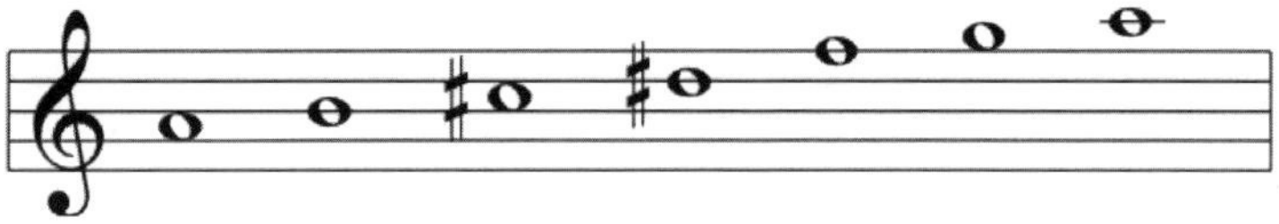

The A whole tone scale consists of only notes that are a whole step apart. There are only seven tones in the whole tone scale, with one letter name omitted.

Example 7

WRITE A CHROMATIC SCALE STARTING ON G, ASCENDING AND DESCENDING, AND EXPLAIN.

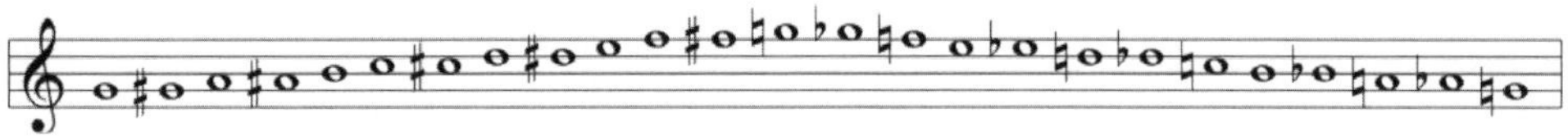

The G chromatic scale consists of only notes that are a half step apart. There are thirteen notes in a chromatic scale. Write the notes ascending in sharps and the notes descending in flats to maintain a systematic approach to writing the chromatic scale.

Example 8

WRITE AN A MIXOLYDIAN MODE AND EXPLAIN.

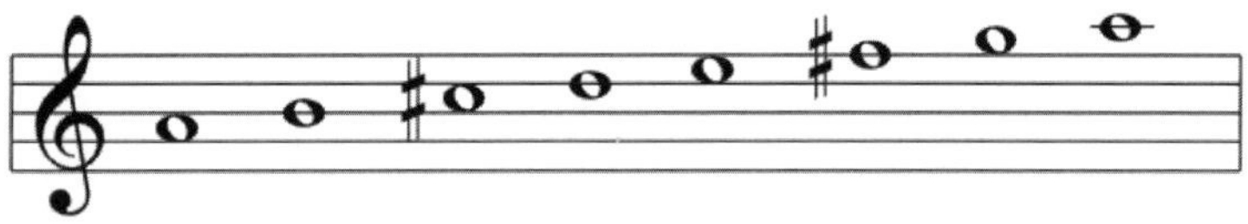

The Mixolydian mode describes a scale series having the following intervals: whole step (W), W, half step (H), W, W, H, and W. In the key of A, the Mixolydian mode produces the scale shown in this measure: A, B, C#, D, E, F#, G, and A.

AUGMENTATION AND EXTENSION OF A PARTICULAR MELODY

Augmentation and extension both refer to melodic devices that alter a given melody. Although both augmentation and extension of a particular melody adds to its overall length, the two motivic devices differ in how they lengthen a given melody. Augmentation refers to the doubling of the rhythmic values of the melodic notes. For example, in a melody that has the note values quarter-quarter-half-eighth-eighth-half-quarter, the augmented form becomes half-half-whole-quarter-quarter-whole-half. Augmentation usually doubles the rhythmic values exactly. Extension refers to the addition of notes to the motive but does not change the rhythmic values. For example, for the melody that follows G-A-B-C, the extended version becomes G-A-G-A-B-A-B-C-D-C-B, where notes are added to the original motive while retaining the notes of the original motive.

Melodic Device Examples

Retrograde Example

Rewrite the Following Melody Using Retrograde.

The melodic device of retrograde takes an original theme or motive and writes the pitches backward; the first note is the last note, and the last note becomes the first note. In the example, the last half note on F becomes the first note followed by the two eighth notes in reverse. The next pitches should follow the original melody backward: F, C, D, E, and ending on the first note, F.

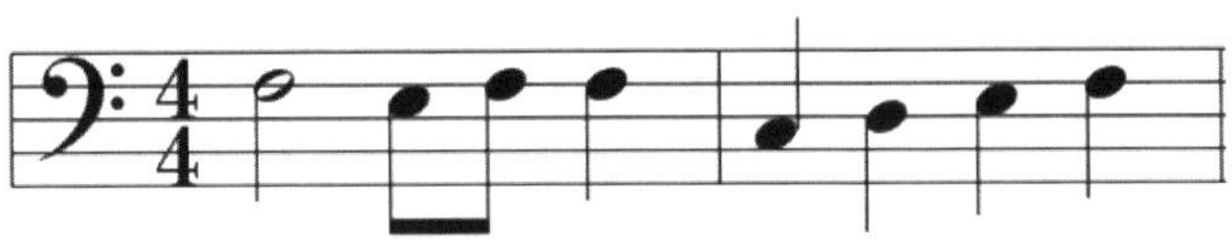

Inversion Example

Rewrite the Following Melody Using Melodic Inversion.

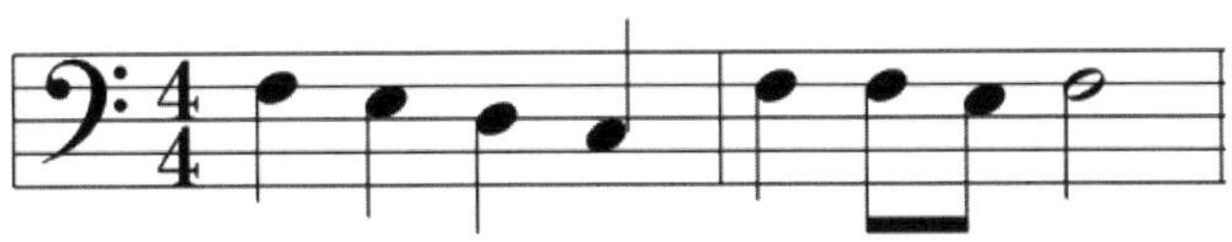

The melodic device of inversion takes an original theme or motive and writes the melody with inverted intervals; that is, if the original theme had a perfect fourth upward, melodic inversion would take that interval downward. In the example, the descending seconds become ascending seconds followed by a downward fourth instead of an upward fourth; repeated notes stay repeated, and the eighth note second from F to E becomes an eighth note second from F to G.

Diminution Example

Rewrite the Following Melody Using Diminution.

The melodic device of diminution takes an original theme or motive and writes the melody with smaller rhythmic values. Diminution typically divides the original rhythmic values in half. In the example, the original quarter notes become eighth notes, eighth notes become sixteenth notes, and the ending half note becomes a quarter note.

Internal Expansion Example

Rewrite the following melody using internal expansion.

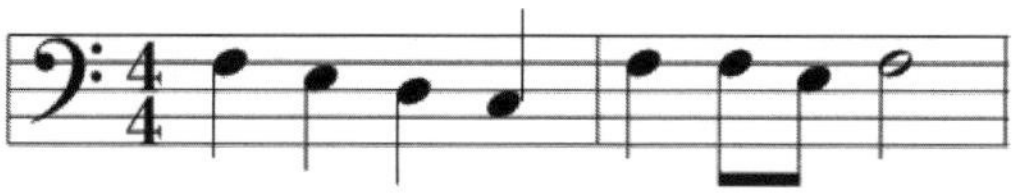

The melodic device of internal expansion takes an original theme or motive and writes the melody with added melodic material to the interior of the motive. In the original two-measure melody, various notes can be added inside the melody; in this case, stepwise eighth notes were added after the downbeat of the second measure to expand the original melody.

Truncation Example

Rewrite the following melody using truncation.

The melodic device of truncation takes an original theme or motive and shortens the melody at the end. The original melody can be shortened at any point. Here, the melody has been truncated after the downbeat of the second measure.

Irregular, Simple, and Compound Meters

Meter refers to the division of rhythm into patterns or pulses within music. Meters can be simple, compound, or irregular. Simple meters are meters that have rhythm divisions of two equal parts, or duple divisions. Time signatures that are simple meters include 2/4, 3/4, and 4/4. All of these time signatures have duple divisions. Compound meters are meters that have rhythmic divisions that can be further subdivided. For example, 6/8 has two pulses per measure, but each pulse can be subdivided into three eighth notes in creating a compound meter. Other compound meters include 9/8 and 12/8. Irregular meters usually have odd numbers as the top number in a time signature, such as the time signature 5/4, which would be grouped as 3+2 or 2+3. Irregular meters can also be simple or compound.

Signature and Meter Type Examples

Example 1

Identify the Following Time Signature and Meter Type.

The time signature for the musical example is 6/8 time signature as there are six eighth-note note values in each measure. This is an example of a compound duple meter with two overall beats that can be subdivided into three smaller beats.

Example 2

Identify the Following Time Signature and Meter Type.

The time signature for the musical example is 9/8 time signature as there are nine eighth-note note values the measure. This is an example of a compound triple meter with three overall beats that can be subdivided into three smaller beats.

Example 3

Identify the Following Time Signature and Meter Type.

The time signature for the musical example is 2/4 time signature as there are two quarter-note note values in each measure. This is an example of a simple duple meter with two basic pulses in each measure.

Example 4

Identify the Following Time Signature and Meter Type.

The time signature for the musical example is 5/4 time signature as there are five quarter-note note values in each measure. This is an example of an irregular or asymmetrical meter with unequal beat groupings.

Example 5

IDENTIFY THE FOLLOWING TIME SIGNATURE AND METER TYPE.

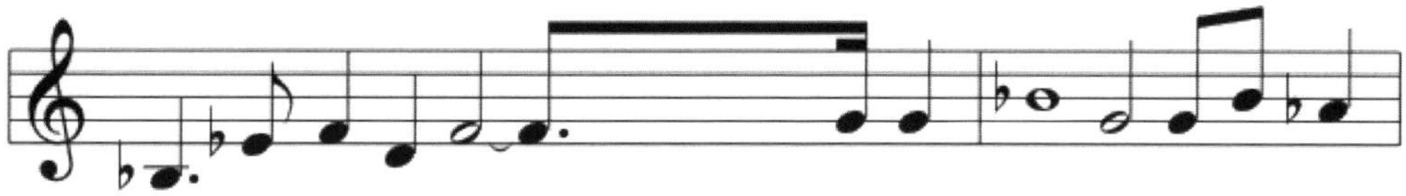

The time signature for the musical example is 4/2 time signature as there are four half-note note values in each measure. This is an example of a simple quadruple meter with four basic pulses in each measure.

RHYTHMIC DEVICE EXAMPLES

Example 1

IDENTIFY THE RHYTHMIC DEVICE USED IN THE SECOND AND THIRD MEASURES OF THE FOLLOWING EXAMPLE.

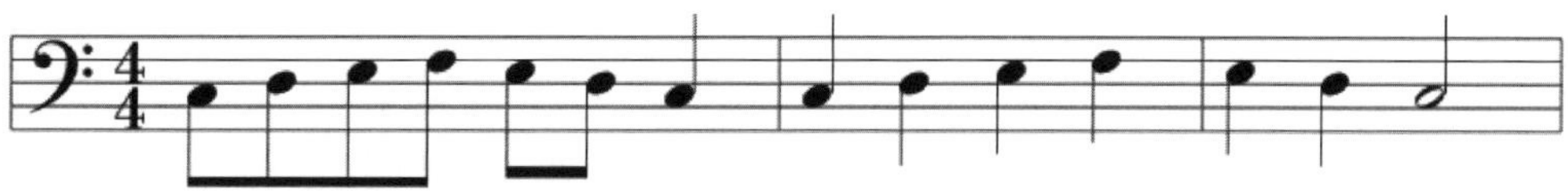

The rhythmic device used in the second and third measures of the example is rhythmic augmentation. The melody from the first measure is repeated, but the note values are doubled from eighth notes to quarter notes and quarter note to half note.

Example 2

IDENTIFY THE RHYTHMIC DEVICE USED IN THE SECOND MEASURE OF THE FOLLOWING EXAMPLE.

The rhythmic device used in the second measure of the example is hemiola. The pulse from the first measure is in two groups of three eighth notes; the second measure changes the rhythmic pulses to three groups of two eighth notes each.

Example 3

IDENTIFY THE RHYTHMIC DEVICE USED IN THE FOLLOWING EXAMPLE.

The rhythmic device used in the example is syncopation. The stress of the pulse falls on the normally weak beats of two and four in common time. Accenting the normally weak beats instead of the normally strong beats purposefully disrupts the natural rhythmic pattern.

Example 4

IDENTIFY THE RHYTHMIC DEVICE USED IN THE THIRD MEASURE OF THE FOLLOWING EXAMPLE.

The rhythmic device used in the third measure of the example is rhythmic diminution. The melody from the first and second measures is repeated, but each of the note values are halved from quarter notes to eighth notes and from half note to quarter note.

POLYPHONY, HOMOPHONY, AND MONOPHONY

The terms *polyphony*, *homophony*, and *monophony* all refer to a certain texture of music. Polyphony refers to a texture of music in which all voices or parts hold similar musical prominence or interest. This can be thought of as several distinct melodic lines occurring at the same time. The rhythm of each line in polyphonic music moves independently of each other. Homophony also has several voices or parts, but melodic interest is reduced to a single voice or part. All other voices or parts support the main melody as accompaniment and move together in rhythmic likeness. In this way, homophony can be thought of as any form of melody and accompaniment texture. Monophony also centers on a single melodic line, however unlike homophony, does not have supplemental accompaniment parts. A prime example of monophony is plainchant, in which a single line of melody embodies the entire work itself.

EQUAL AND UNEQUAL VOICE POLYPHONY

The term *polyphony* refers to the texture of any music that is made up of many equally important melodic lines. Examples include much of Renaissance and Baroque music. Within polyphony, there exists equal- and unequal-voice polyphony. Equal-voice polyphony refers to polyphony that maintains the same thematic material in all the individual voices. A prime example of equal-voice polyphony is the canon, in which the exact same melodic material enters sequentially after a uniform time interval. Other examples of equal-voice polyphony include fugues, inventions, and other forms of imitation. Unequal-voice polyphony refers to polyphony in which greater importance is given to one or more melodic lines. Examples of unequal-voice polyphony include Medieval-era cantus firmus compositions that give musical precedence to the cantus firmus, usually sung or played in the tenor voice.

ACCOMPANIMENT EXAMPLE

Example 1

DESCRIBE THE TYPE OF BASS ACCOMPANIMENT IN THE FOLLOWING MUSICAL EXAMPLE.

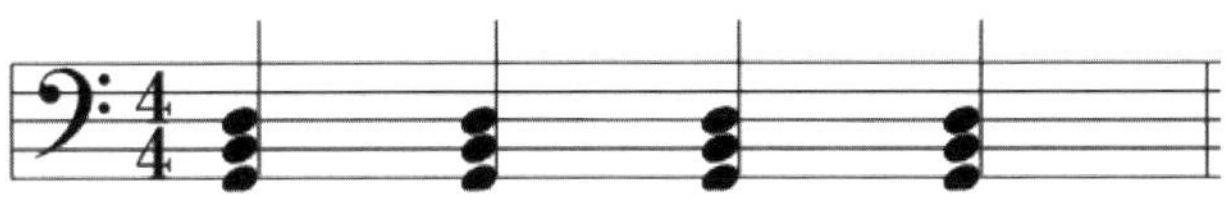

The type of bass accompaniment in the musical example is chordal accompaniment. This accompaniment pattern uses blocked chords, such as the G chord in the example, in providing harmonic support to a melody.

Difference Between a Tonal and Real Answer to a Fugal Subject

The fugue is a form of imitative counterpoint in which a fugue theme is introduced at the beginning of the work, also known as the exposition, and is echoed in all of the fugal voices though imitation and development. The term *fugue* comes from the Latin *fugere* meaning, "to flee," as each voice essentially chases the previous voice. The initial subject is called the leader, or *dux*, and is presented in the tonic key. The *dux* is usually followed by the *comes*, the companion answer in the dominant key, which can be presented in one of two ways: real or tonal. In a real answer to a fugal subject, the theme is transposed exactly note to note in the dominant key. In a tonal answer to a fugal subject, the theme is transposed loosely in the dominant key, modified so as to maintain harmonic congruity or to facilitate modulations.

Example 2

Describe the Type of Bass Accompaniment in the Following Musical Example.

The type of bass accompaniment in the musical example is Alberti bass. This accompaniment pattern uses a broken chord pattern of 1-5-3-5 of the chord tones in providing harmonic support to a melody.

Example 3

Describe the Type of Bass Accompaniment in the Following Musical Example.

The type of bass accompaniment in the musical example is a walking bass. This accompaniment pattern uses a steady rhythmic pattern of moving single notes in providing harmonic support to a melody.

General Components of Basic Phrase Structure (Period, Antecedent, and Consequent)

A phrase is defined as a musical statement in which there is some aspect of completeness, harmonic movement, and tension and release. A typical phrase is four measures in length, although many are not four measures in length. When two or more phrases are combined, they create periods. A period usually contains two phrases: an antecedent question phrase and a consequent answer phrase. The antecedent phrase usually ends on an incomplete cadence such as the half cadence or deceptive cadence. It creates a sense of a question because it is incomplete. The consequent phrase usually ends on a complete phrase, such as the authentic cadence, to provide a sense of an answer with its definitive ending. The typical period is eight measures long, consisting of two four-measure phrases.

Contrasting and Parallel Periods

A period is formed when two phrases are combined in an antecedent question phrase and a consequent answer phrase. Contrasting periods are periods in which the antecedent phrase and the consequent phrase contain different harmonic or motivic material. The phrase form of contrasting periods can be described as ab. Parallel periods are periods in which the antecedent phrase and the consequent phrase contain similar harmonic or motivic material. The phrase form of parallel periods can be described as aa. The first phrase in both contrasting and parallel periods usually ends on a weak cadence, whereas the second phrase ends on a strong cadence to create the period.

Double Period

A period is formed when two phrases are combined in an antecedent question phrase and a consequent answer phrase. A double period occurs when two periods are combined to take on the role of antecedent period and consequent period with a total of four phrases. The first and third phrases are usually similar musically in its melodies and harmonies. The second phrase usually ends in an incomplete cadence such as the half cadence, deceptive cadence, or imperfect cadence, whereas the fourth phrase ends with a complete cadence such as the perfect authentic cadence. A double period implies a weak cadence at the end of the first period and a strong cadence at the end of the second period.

Phrase Groups and Phrase Chains

A phrase is defined as a musical statement in which there is some aspect of completeness, harmonic movement, and tension and release. A typical phrase is four measures in length, although many are not four measures in length. When three or more phrases are combined, they create phase groups and phrase chains. A phrase group has three or more phrases, with at least two of them similar so that it can be described as aab or abb form. The first two usually end with incomplete cadences like the half, deceptive, or imperfect cadence, whereas the last one usually ends with a complete cadence, such as the perfect authentic cadence. A phrase chain also has three of more phrases, but all of them have contrasting musical material. The last phrase also ends with a conclusive cadence.

Phrase Elision

Phrase elision occurs when two phrases overlap. The cadence of the first phrase occurs simultaneously with the beginning of the second phrase so that the last measure of the first phrase is also the first measure of the second phrase. In phrase elision, the end of the first phrase is typically omitted so that the second phrase can begin in its place as a recognizable beginning of the second phrase. For example, a phrase that usually ends with a whole note A in 4/4 time begins instead with the sixteenth note motive of the second phrase, which continues on from the point of elision. In this scheme, the two four-measure phrases become a complete seven-measure section instead of eight measures.

A and B Sections of Binary Form

Binary form refers to a structure of a piece in which there are two main sections of musical material, labeled A and B. They are usually of similar length and are usually both repeated. If the work is in a major key, the A section starts in the tonic key and ends in the dominant key, whereas the B section begins in the dominant key and ends in the tonic. If the work is in a minor key, the A section starts in the tonic key and ends either in the dominant key or the relative major key; the B section begins in either the dominant key or the relative major key and ends in the tonic. The musical content of both the A and B section generally contains similar musical material and does not contrast greatly.

Rounded Binary and Ternary Form

The structure of rounded binary and ternary forms both contain three contrasting sections. The first section can be described as the A section with its introductory thematic musical material, a contrasting B section, and a certain amount of the beginning A section at the end. In ternary form, the beginning A section ends on tonic with a perfect authentic cadence; in a rounded binary form, however, the beginning A section can end on tonic with a perfect authentic cadence, as in ternary form, or it can also end on the dominant either through modulation or through a half cadence. The B section of a rounded binary form is always in the dominant key; in ternary form, however, the B section is a new key with new musical material as well. In ternary form, the third section is always a complete return of the A section; in rounded binary form, however, the return of the A is incomplete and is usually a phrase or motive and insufficient to claim the A label and thus the "rounding."

Composition

Compositions can sometimes begin with musical material before the main exposition; this material is called the introduction and can be as short as a few measures or as long as an entire movement in a larger work. An introduction does not contain any thematic material and therefore is not usually repeated if the exposition is repeated. Musical elements from the introduction may reappear elsewhere in the work but not as the introductory whole. An introduction prepares the music for the exposition and presents a smooth transition into the thematic material. Introductions can also be presented as a contrasting element to the thematic material, for example, a slow introduction to a fast exposition. Introductions can also mark the opening of the music as a call to attention, as in a series of loud trumpet calls.

Theme

In the musical form theme and variations, theme is clearly stated in the beginning. Each section that follows is a variation of the theme where the musical material is slightly altered each time through texture, harmony, rhythm, and character. The variations may be a simple change of the key or accompaniment or as complex as fragmented melodies that may not be easily recognizable as the original thematic material. Other variation tools include ornamentation, simplification, and additive processes. Theme and variations are usually performed as a whole composition without stopping. Theme and variations can be open, in which each section flows into the next one without closure, or closed, in which each section has a definitive closure.

Simple and Compound Musical Form

Simple musical form describes a tonal work that can be seen as a complete and self-contained work that is not divisible into other, smaller self-contained works. Examples of simple musical forms include binary and ternary forms. In each of these forms, there are thematic sections labeled A or B, but neither of these thematic sections can be further divisible into other simple forms. Compound musical form describes a tonal work that can be seen as a composite form that is made up of other, smaller, simple forms such as binary and ternary forms. An example of a compound form is the Minuetto and Trio, in which the simple Minuetto form surrounds the simple binary Trio form to create an overall ternary compound form. Other examples of compound musical forms are sonata movements, symphony movements, string quartets, and suites.

AP Practice Test

Want to take this practice test in an online interactive format?
Check out the online resources page, which includes interactive practice questions and much more: **mometrix.com/resources719/apmusictheory**

Multiple Choice

The AP Music Theory test contains questions with aural stimulus as well as questions without aural stimulus. The questions contained in this practice test represent the portion of the test without aural stimulus.

1. What occurs when the rhythmic pattern changes from pulses of two to two pulses of three?

a. Hemiola
b. Syncopation
c. Augmentation
d. Agogic accent

2. Identify the following pitch:

a. B
b. D
c. E
d. C

3. In a fugue, what is a tonal answer?

a. An exact restatement of the subject
b. An exact transposition of the subject
c. A transposition of the subject with intervallic adjustments
d. A transposition of the subject with rhythmic adjustments

4. What is the following mode?

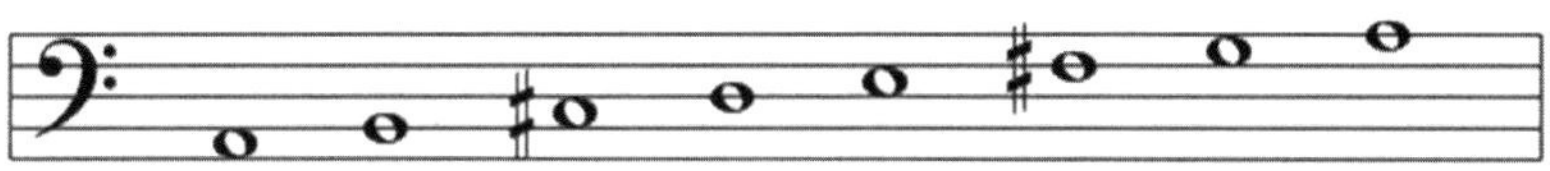

a. Mixolydian
b. Lydian
c. Phrygian
d. Dorian

5. What is an accompaniment that uses solid or blocked chords?

a. Walking bass
b. Chordal accompaniment
c. Alberti bass
d. Ostinato

6. What is the term for polyphony based on the same thematic material?

a. Non-imitative polyphony
b. Polyphonic texture
c. Counterpoint
d. Imitative polyphony

7. What is the correct Roman numeral analysis for the following example?

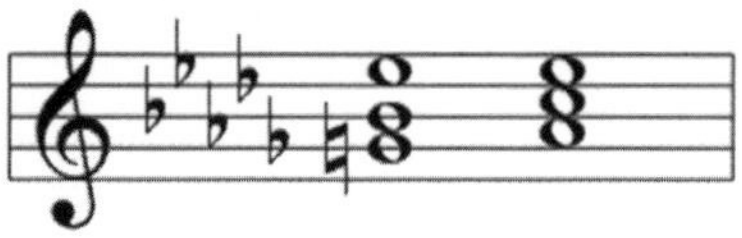

a. V7 – I Perfect cadence in Db Major
b. V6/V – V Half cadence in Db Major
c. Vb5 – vi deceptive cadence in Bb minor
d. IV/vi – I Plagal cadence in Bb minor

8. What is the musical term that means "stolen"?

a. Volare
b. Rubato
c. Tutti
d. Ostinato

9. What is the following key signature?

a. Cb Major
b. Db Major
c. Gb Major
d. Fb Major

10. What is the definition for "pizzicato"?

a. Pluck the strings
b. Strike the strings
c. Bow the strings
d. Snap the strings

11. What word means that a part or section is essential and must be played, according to most historical interpretations?

a. Timbre
b. Soli
c. Obbligato
d. Tutti

12. What instrument group does the tom-tom belong to?

a. Strings
b. Percussion
c. Woodwinds
d. Brass

13. Which instrument is used to realize a continuo part?

a. Clarinet
b. Snare drum
c. Upright bass
d. Keyboard

14. What is the following ornament?

a. Mordent
b. Trill
c. Appogiatura
d. Turn

15. Which term describes a melody that is repeated backwards?

a. Countermelody
b. Retrograde
c. Augmentation
d. Sequence

16. What does internal expansion refer to?

a. Notes that are added to the end of a melody
b. Notes that are doubled in value in a melody
c. Notes that are added to the beginning of a melody
d. Notes that are added to the middle of a melody

17. Which chord does NOT act with a pre-dominant function?

a. vi
b. ii
c. I
d. IV

18. What is the type of phrase structure in which two phrases overlap?

a. Parallel period
b. Elision
c. Antecedent/consequent
d. Phrase group

19. Which of the following best describes the melody below?

a. Embellished
b. Imitative
c. Conjunct
d. Disjunct

20. Which describes music that moves in an unexpected harmonic progression?

a. Deceptive progression
b. Retrogression
c. Phrase modulation
d. Retrograde

21. What is the following key signature?

a. G# minor
b. D# minor
c. A# minor
d. E# minor

22. What is the definition of tonicization?

a. Long key changes for many phrases
b. Short key change for repeated measures
c. Long key change for a section
d. Short key change for only a few measures

23. Which of the following harmonic progressions is a common chord progression?

a. I-IV
b. I-ii
c. I-vi
d. I-vii

24. Which of the following harmonic progressions is a rare chord progression?

a. IV-V
b. ii-V
c. V-I
d. I-ii

25. Which describes the rise and fall of a melody?

a. Sequence
b. Repetition
c. Contour
d. Countermelody

26. What is the time signature for the following example?

a. 6/4
b. 3/8
c. 6/8
d. 3/4

27. Which describes the harmonic function of neighboring 6/4 chords?

a. All notes in the chord move to a neighbor note.
b. The bass stays the same while the other notes move stepwise to a new harmony.
c. The alto stays the same while the other notes move stepwise to a new harmony.
d. The soprano and bass stay the same while the inner voices move stepwise to a new harmony.

28. Voices that move in opposite directions are described by which term?

a. Parallel motion
b. Oblique motion
c. Similar motion
d. Contrary motion

29. When writing first inversion ii, iii, iv, and vi chords in four-part harmony, which note is the best note to double?

a. Fifth
b. Root
c. Third
d. The soprano note

30. What is the interval shown in the example?

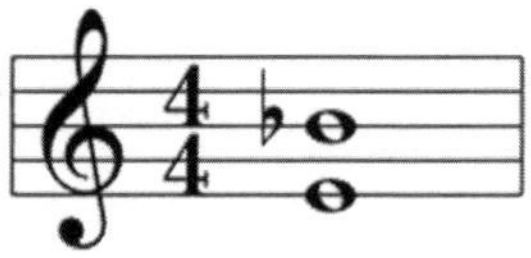

a. Augmented fifth
b. Diminished fifth
c. Perfect fifth
d. Major fifth

31. Which harmonic function is considered to have the strongest function?

a. Tonic function
b. Dominant function
c. Pre-dominant function
d. Post-dominant function

32. What is the Roman numeral analysis for the following harmony?

a. vii°/iii chord in A Major
b. V/vi chord in E# Major
c. ii°/VI chord in C# minor
d. vii°/IV chord in B Major

33. Which describes the nonharmonic tone that is held into a new harmony and resolved downward by step?

a. Retardation
b. Suspension
c. Preparation
d. Ostinato

34. In a sonata, the scherzo or minuet movement is typically in which form?

a. Binary
b. Rondo
c. Ternary
d. Theme and variations

35. The following example contains which part-writing error?

a. Crossed voices
b. Hidden fifths
c. Parallel octaves
d. Voice exchange

36. What does the symbol F° indicate?

a. F diminished
b. F minor
c. F augmented
d. F major

37. What is heterophony?

a. Several different parts that each have melodic interest
b. A single line with no accompaniment
c. One line acts as the melody with other lines as accompaniment
d. Two or more lines that have the same melody with slight variations

38. Which of the following harmonic progressions is a deceptive cadence?

a. V-I
b. V-vi
c. I-V
d. IV-I

39. The V7-I harmonic progression is which of the following cadences?

a. Half cadence
b. Deceptive cadence
c. Authentic cadence
d. Plagal cadence

Questions 40-46 are based on the excerpt below from Beethoven's Minuet No. 5, WoO 10.

40. The musical excerpt above is in which key?

a. D Major
b. B minor
c. D minor
d. B Major

41. The non-chord tone in measures 1-2 is what type of non-chord tone?

a. Ostinato
b. Appogiatura
c. Neighbor note
d. Pedal point

42. In measures 4-8, the music modulates to which key?

a. E major
b. B minor
c. A Major
d. F# minor

43. Measure 12 has what type of cadence?

a. Authentic cadence
b. Plagal cadence
c. Deceptive cadence
d. Half cadence

44. Measures 9-11 do NOT contain which motivic device?

a. Truncation
b. Sequence
c. Fragmentation
d. Retrograde

45. What is the harmony in measure 10, beat 1?

a. B dominant 7
b. D# diminished 7
c. A dominant 7
d. D# dominant 7

46. What is the Roman numeral analysis for measure 4?

a. I
b. V
c. IV
d. vi

47. What is the term that describes two ensembles that alternate parts?

a. Antiphonal
b. Polyphonic
c. Strophic
d. Chordal

48. What is the sonata allegro form?

a. Exposition, denouement, recapitulation
b. Exposition, development, recapitulation
c. Explication, development, recapitulation
d. Explication, denouement, recapitulation

49. What is the term for an extended ending that is not part of the standard form?

a. Codetta
b. De capo
c. Coda
d. Al segno

50. A song that is through-composed has...

a. A different melody for each verse.
b. The same melody for each verse.
c. The same music and words for each verse.
d. The same melody for each verse but varied.

Written Free Response Section

1. Realize the figured bass for the following example. Use four voices following the 18th century practices of four-part writing. Write in the Roman numeral below each chord.

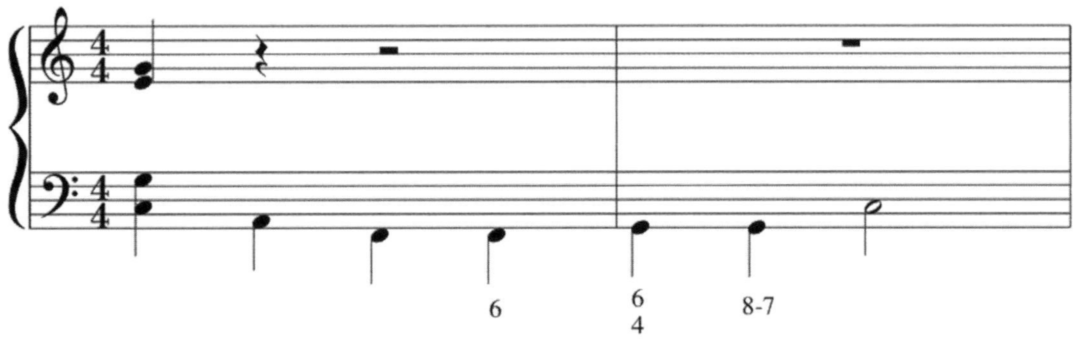

2. Complete the following harmonic progression in four voices following the 18th century practices of four-part writing. Use only quarter notes and half notes.

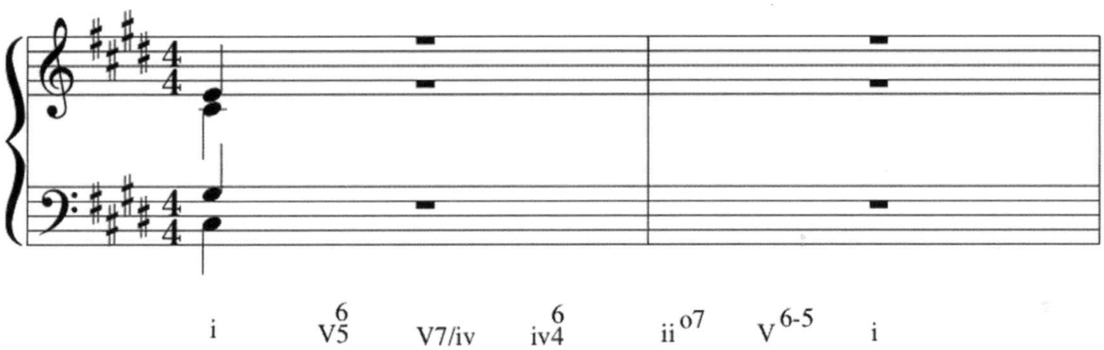

3. Write the bass line to the following melody and add Roman numerals for the implied harmonies.

Sight-Singing Selections

1.

2.

Answer and Explanations

Multiple Choice

1. A: Hemiola occurs when the pulsing rhythm changes from pulses of two to three or pulses of three to two. For example, in a 6/8 time signature, a pulsing pattern of six eighth notes changes to three quarter notes in which the grouped pattern becomes two eighth notes instead of three.

2. D: The clef pictured is the alto clef, which uses the C clef with two curves that meet in the center and two lines to the left of it. The point where the curves meet is C. For the alto clef, the C clef rests on the third line; therefore, the note pictured which is on the third line of the staff is C.

3. C: In a tonal answer to a fugal subject, the theme is transposed loosely in the dominant key, modified so as to maintain harmonic congruity or to facilitate modulations. Therefore, the answer is C, a transposition of the subject with intervallic adjustments. It doesn't pertain to rhythm and cannot be an exact restatement of the subject or an exact transposition of the subject.

4. A: The scale pictured has the following pattern of: starting pitch – whole step – whole step – half step – whole step – whole step – half step – whole step. The half steps occur between scale degrees three and four, and scale degrees six and seven. The mode pictured is the Mixolydian mode.

5. B: The type of bass accompaniment that uses solid or blocked chords is chordal accompaniment. This accompaniment pattern uses blocked chords such as the G chord to provide harmonic support to a melody. Walking and Alberti bass feature one note at a time while ostinato does not necessarily use chords.

6. D: Polyphony based on the same thematic material is imitative polyphony in which the same musical ideas are used throughout the composition. Imitation is used between the voices, as well as in each line. Examples of imitative polyphony include canon, fugal imitation, and strict imitation.

7. B: In the musical example, the key signature indicates Db Major. The first chord is Eb major in first inversion, a nondiatonic chord in the key. The second chord is Ab major in root position. In the key of Db Major, the second is the dominant V chord, and the first Eb chord is the dominant V chord in Ab major, so the correct answer is B: V6/V – V Half cadence in Db Major.

8. B: The musical term that means "stolen" is B: rubato. The term means to play expressively and manipulate the tempo by "stealing" time: speeding up and slowing down the tempo of a musical performance according to interpretation. "Volare" means to fly, "tutti" means all, and "ostinato" means stubborn or persistent.

9. C: To determine a flat key signature, take the penultimate flat; that is the key signature because each added flat is a fourth apart. In this example, the last two flats are Gb and Cb; the next to last flat is Gb, so the key is in Gb. The correct answer is C: Gb Major.

10. A: "Pizzicato" means to pluck a stringed instrument. The musical term comes from the Italian *pizzicare*, which means to pluck, pinch, or nip. When playing a musical passage with pizzicato, plucking a stringed instrument produces a sound that has a sharper attack.

11. C: The word that means that a part or section must be played is obbligato. In certain periods of musical interpretation, the meaning has been inverted to mean optional. In the 18th century, the

term meant that a section or part must be played. In the 19th century, the term meant that a part could be omitted.

12. B: The tom-tom belongs to the percussion family. It is a drum that has no snares and is a standard part of a drum kit. Tom-toms commonly range between six and 20 inches in diameter and eight to 13 inches in depth. Tom-toms can be played hanging on a stand or on the floor.

13. D: The instrument used to realize a continuo part is the keyboard. Figured bass is closely tied with the accompaniment continuo part, and the keyboard is able to provide the notated bass part as well as the other voices based on the numbers provided by the figured bass.

14. D: The ornament pictured is a turn. As a non-harmonic performance direction, ornaments are tones that are not contained within a certain harmony. A turn is performed by playing the note above the written note, the written note, the note below it, and then returning to the written note.

15. B: The term that describes a melody that is repeated backwards is retrograde. The melodic device of retrograde takes an original theme or motive and writes the pitches backwards; the first note is the last note, and the last note becomes the first note.

16. D: Internal expansion refers to notes that are added to the middle of a melody. It serves to lengthen a thematic motive. Internal expansion refers to additional melodic material that is added within the original theme or motive and commonly utilizes elements of repetition, sequence, and augmentation, to add length within a motive.

17. C: The tonic I chord does not serve a pre-dominant function; it acts as the only chord with a tonic function. The pre-dominant function serves as the move away from the foundational tonic and as a preparation for dominant chords. Pre-dominant function creates variety and interest in the moments between tonic and dominant functions.

18. B: The type of phrase structure in which two phrases overlap is elision. In phrase elision, the cadence of the first phrase occurs simultaneously with the beginning of the second phrase so that the last measure of the first phrase is also the first measure of the second phrase.

19. D: The term that best describes the pictured melody is D: disjunct. The term refers to the wide movement of the pitches within a melody. A disjunct melody moves primarily by leaps rather than by steps. In the pictured melody, the melody moves primarily by large leaps rather than by steps.

20. A: Deceptive progression describes music that moves in an unexpected harmonic progression. A deceptive progression, also known as a deceptive cadence, often moves from a dominant V to the submediant vi. Aurally, the effect is that of surprise since the expectation when hearing the dominant V is for the V to resolve to the I chord; instead, the cadence deceives the ear, thus the term deceptive progression.

21. B: To determine a sharp key signature, take the last sharp in the key signature and raise it by a half step to find the major key. For the minor key, take the major key and count down three half steps. In the pictured example, the key signature has the last sharp as E#; a half step up finds the major key as F# Major. The relative minor key is three half steps lower, or D# minor.

22. D: Tonicization is a short key change, for only a few measures. The new key is established through harmonic movement and cadences. Tonicization commonly uses key relationships such as closely related keys, enharmonically equivalent keys, and parallel keys.

23. A: I-IV is a common harmonic chord progression. The tonic to subdominant movement is often used as a step away from the home key in preparation for the dominant. Tonic to supertonic, tonic to submediant, and tonic to the leading tone are all less common harmonic chord progressions.

24. D: I-ii is a rare harmonic chord progression. The tonic usually moves to the more common subdominant function of the IV chord. The chord progressions subdominant to dominant, supertonic to dominant, and dominant to tonic are all much more common harmonic chord progressions.

25. C: Contour describes the rise and fall of a melody; it refers to the movement of the pitches, whether ascending or descending, near or far. Words that describe the contour of a melody include conjunct, disjunct, terraced, arc contour, and undulating contour.

26. C: The time signature for the musical example is 6/8 time signature since there are six eighth-note note values in each measure. This is an example of a compound duple meter with two overall beats that can be subdivided into three smaller beats. None of the other time signatures fit with the number of counts given.

27. B: In the harmonic function of neighboring 6/4 chords, the bass stays the same while the other notes move stepwise to a new harmony. Also known as the pedal 6/4, the neighboring 6/4 chord is found between two tonic chords as the third and fifth of the chord move to and from their neighbor notes.

28. D: Voices that move in opposite directions are considered to move in contrary motion. Similar motion refers to voices that move in the same direction but not necessarily by the same intervals. Oblique motion refers to voice movement where one voice stays the same and the other voice moves. Parallel motion refers to voices that move by the same direction and intervals.

29. C: When writing first inversion ii, iii, iv, and vi chords in four-part harmony, the best note to double is the third. This allows for the best voice leading because the third note acts as the bass note in first inversion chords while allowing proper voice leading movement in the upper three voices.

30. B: The interval shown in the example is a diminished fifth. Counting every line and space between and including the two notes makes a fifth. E to B is a perfect fifth with seven half steps. Since the fifth is made smaller by a half step to only six half steps, the interval is a diminished fifth.

31. A: The harmonic function considered to have the strongest function is the tonic function. The tonic function serves as the strongest chord that defines the key of a piece of music. It is the sense of home and resolution in the music, and usually the end goal of the harmonic progression.

32. A: The Roman numeral analysis for the following harmony is the vii°/iii chord in A Major. The chord in the example is a B# diminished triad, a leading tone chord that resolves to tonic. In this case, the chord should resolve to C# as the tonic. Of the secondary dominants, C# is the iii chord in the key of A Major.

33. B: The nonharmonic tone that is held into a new harmony and resolved downward by step is the suspension. A retardation note describes a dissonance that is held over and resolved by an upward step. A preparation is a chord tone that precedes a dissonant note. An ostinato is repeated pattern that is constant in the bass voice.

34. C: In a sonata, the scherzo or minuet movement is typically in ternary form. The four movements typical in a sonata are the allegro, adagio, scherzo or minuet, and the allegro. The scherzo or minuet form usually has a trio that follows so that the form is performed ABA.

35. C: The pictured example contains the part-writing error of parallel octaves. The soprano and bass lines are doubled incorrectly in creating the parallel octaves that move from G to A. This is considered to be an objectionable parallel and should be avoided in four-part HARMONY.

36. A: The symbol "F°" indicates an F diminished chord. An F minor chord would be indicated as "f" or an abbreviated "F min." F augmented would be indicated as "F+." F Major would be indicated as "F" or an abbreviated "F Maj."

37. D: Heterophony is two or more lines that have the same melody with slight variations. Usually there are two or more performers that sing the lines simultaneously. Variations include ornaments, passing tones, neighbor tones, and other types of variations.

38. B: The harmonic progression that is a deceptive cadence is V-vi. A deceptive cadence is defined as any cadence that moves from a dominant V to the submediant vi instead of the usual movement of dominant V to tonic I. Aurally, the effect is that of surprise since the expectation when hearing the dominant V is for the dominant to resolve to the tonic chord.

39. C: The V7-I harmonic progression is an authentic cadence. The authentic cadence is defined as a dominant sounding harmony resolving to the tonic harmony, notated as V-I, V7-I, V-i, or V7-i in Western tonal theory. The authentic cadence is considered to be the strongest cadence because of the supertonic and the leading tone.

40. A: The musical excerpt is in D major. The two sharps of the key signature indicate either D major or B minor. To determine whether the musical excerpt is in the major or minor key, look for the tonic harmony in the beginning as well as at the end. In this excerpt, the tonic is D major.

41. D: The non-chord tone in measures 1-2 is a pedal point. A pedal point is a non-harmonic tone that is sustained for an extended amount of time. Unlike other non-harmonic tones, pedal points usually start as a consonant note that, when held, become dissonant with the moving parts until it is resolved back to a consonant note with the other voices.

42. C: In measures 4-8, the music modulates to A major. As in the opening theme, the pedal point is A, or the fifth scale degree in D major. In measures 4-8, the pedal point is E, or the fifth scale degree in A major. There is also an authentic cadence in measure 8 from E major to A major.

43. D: Measure 12 has a half cadence. The harmonies on beats one and two are D major to A major. At this point in the excerpt, the music is in D major, thus the Roman numeric analysis of I-V. The half cadence is defined as any harmony progressing to a dominant harmony.

44. D: Measures 9-11 do not contain the motivic device of retrograde. The melodic device of retrograde takes an original theme or motive and writes the pitches backwards; the first note is the last note, and the last note becomes the first note. Measures 9-11 contain truncation, sequence, and fragmentation.

45. A: The harmony in measure 10, beat 1 is a B dominant 7. The pitches present are D#, F#, A, and B. Rearranged in order from root to seventh, the pitches are B, D#, F#, and A. The harmony has a lower major triad with a minor seventh interval making the chord a B dominant 7.

46. B: The Roman numeral analysis for measure 4 is V. The pitches found in the measure 4 are A, C#, and E, which make up the A major triad. In the key of D major, A is the fifth scale degree, which makes the Roman numeral analysis the dominant V chord.

47. A: The term that describes two ensembles with alternating parts is antiphonal. Antiphonal music stems from the antiphon and refers to a call and response style of singing in which two choirs or two sections of the choir alternate parts. Antiphonal music can also be described as polychoral music.

48. B: The sonata allegro form is exposition, development, and recapitulation. The exposition establishes the theme as well as the key of the form. In the development section, the theme is freely manipulated. In the recapitulation, the themes from the exposition reappear, but are both in the tonic key this time.

49. C: The term for an extended ending that is not part of the standard form is the coda. A coda is usually found at the end of an entire composition and is not made up of the thematic material. It serves to reinforce the cadence at the end in its finality.

50. A: A song that is through-composed has a different melody for each verse. Through-composed music tends to be more complex. In through-composed music, the music feels much more continuous without clear verse breaks and has a sense of musical as well as lyrical development.

Written Free Response Section

1. A possible answer is as follows:

2. A possible answer is as follows:

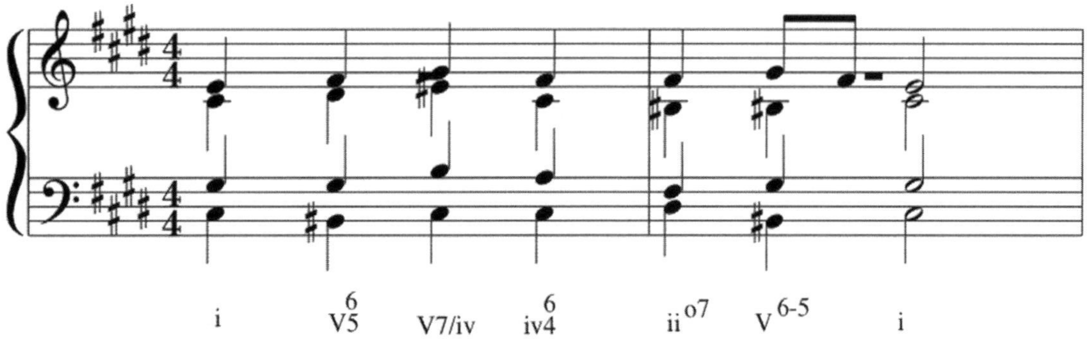

3. A possible answer is as follows:

How to Overcome Test Anxiety

Just the thought of taking a test is enough to make most people a little nervous. A test is an important event that can have a long-term impact on your future, so it's important to take it seriously and it's natural to feel anxious about performing well. But just because anxiety is normal, that doesn't mean that it's helpful in test taking, or that you should simply accept it as part of your life. Anxiety can have a variety of effects. These effects can be mild, like making you feel slightly nervous, or severe, like blocking your ability to focus or remember even a simple detail.

If you experience test anxiety—whether severe or mild—it's important to know how to beat it. To discover this, first you need to understand what causes test anxiety.

Causes of Test Anxiety

While we often think of anxiety as an uncontrollable emotional state, it can actually be caused by simple, practical things. One of the most common causes of test anxiety is that a person does not feel adequately prepared for their test. This feeling can be the result of many different issues such as poor study habits or lack of organization, but the most common culprit is time management. Starting to study too late, failing to organize your study time to cover all of the material, or being distracted while you study will mean that you're not well prepared for the test. This may lead to cramming the night before, which will cause you to be physically and mentally exhausted for the test. Poor time management also contributes to feelings of stress, fear, and hopelessness as you realize you are not well prepared but don't know what to do about it.

Other times, test anxiety is not related to your preparation for the test but comes from unresolved fear. This may be a past failure on a test, or poor performance on tests in general. It may come from comparing yourself to others who seem to be performing better or from the stress of living up to expectations. Anxiety may be driven by fears of the future—how failure on this test would affect your educational and career goals. These fears are often completely irrational, but they can still negatively impact your test performance.

Elements of Test Anxiety

As mentioned earlier, test anxiety is considered to be an emotional state, but it has physical and mental components as well. Sometimes you may not even realize that you are suffering from test anxiety until you notice the physical symptoms. These can include trembling hands, rapid heartbeat, sweating, nausea, and tense muscles. Extreme anxiety may lead to fainting or vomiting. Obviously, any of these symptoms can have a negative impact on testing. It is important to recognize them as soon as they begin to occur so that you can address the problem before it damages your performance.

The mental components of test anxiety include trouble focusing and inability to remember learned information. During a test, your mind is on high alert, which can help you recall information and stay focused for an extended period of time. However, anxiety interferes with your mind's natural processes, causing you to blank out, even on the questions you know well. The strain of testing during anxiety makes it difficult to stay focused, especially on a test that may take several hours. Extreme anxiety can take a huge mental toll, making it difficult not only to recall test information but even to understand the test questions or pull your thoughts together.

Effects of Test Anxiety

Test anxiety is like a disease—if left untreated, it will get progressively worse. Anxiety leads to poor performance, and this reinforces the feelings of fear and failure, which in turn lead to poor performances on subsequent tests. It can grow from a mild nervousness to a crippling condition. If allowed to progress, test anxiety can have a big impact on your schooling, and consequently on your future.

Test anxiety can spread to other parts of your life. Anxiety on tests can become anxiety in any stressful situation, and blanking on a test can turn into panicking in a job situation. But fortunately, you don't have to let anxiety rule your testing and determine your grades. There are a number of relatively simple steps you can take to move past anxiety and function normally on a test and in the rest of life.

Physical Steps for Beating Test Anxiety

While test anxiety is a serious problem, the good news is that it can be overcome. It doesn't have to control your ability to think and remember information. While it may take time, you can begin taking steps today to beat anxiety.

Just as your first hint that you may be struggling with anxiety comes from the physical symptoms, the first step to treating it is also physical. Rest is crucial for having a clear, strong mind. If you are tired, it is much easier to give in to anxiety. But if you establish good sleep habits, your body and mind will be ready to perform optimally, without the strain of exhaustion. Additionally, sleeping well helps you to retain information better, so you're more likely to recall the answers when you see the test questions.

Getting good sleep means more than going to bed on time. It's important to allow your brain time to relax. Take study breaks from time to time so it doesn't get overworked, and don't study right before bed. Take time to rest your mind before trying to rest your body, or you may find it difficult to fall asleep.

Along with sleep, other aspects of physical health are important in preparing for a test. Good nutrition is vital for good brain function. Sugary foods and drinks may give a burst of energy but this burst is followed by a crash, both physically and emotionally. Instead, fuel your body with protein and vitamin-rich foods.

Also, drink plenty of water. Dehydration can lead to headaches and exhaustion, especially if your brain is already under stress from the rigors of the test. Particularly if your test is a long one, drink water during the breaks. And if possible, take an energy-boosting snack to eat between sections.

Along with sleep and diet, a third important part of physical health is exercise. Maintaining a steady workout schedule is helpful, but even taking 5-minute study breaks to walk can help get your blood pumping faster and clear your head. Exercise also releases endorphins, which contribute to a positive feeling and can help combat test anxiety.

When you nurture your physical health, you are also contributing to your mental health. If your body is healthy, your mind is much more likely to be healthy as well. So take time to rest, nourish your body with healthy food and water, and get moving as much as possible. Taking these physical steps will make you stronger and more able to take the mental steps necessary to overcome test anxiety.

Mental Steps for Beating Test Anxiety

Working on the mental side of test anxiety can be more challenging, but as with the physical side, there are clear steps you can take to overcome it. As mentioned earlier, test anxiety often stems from lack of preparation, so the obvious solution is to prepare for the test. Effective studying may be the most important weapon you have for beating test anxiety, but you can and should employ several other mental tools to combat fear.

First, boost your confidence by reminding yourself of past success—tests or projects that you aced. If you're putting as much effort into preparing for this test as you did for those, there's no reason you should expect to fail here. Work hard to prepare; then trust your preparation.

Second, surround yourself with encouraging people. It can be helpful to find a study group, but be sure that the people you're around will encourage a positive attitude. If you spend time with others who are anxious or cynical, this will only contribute to your own anxiety. Look for others who are motivated to study hard from a desire to succeed, not from a fear of failure.

Third, reward yourself. A test is physically and mentally tiring, even without anxiety, and it can be helpful to have something to look forward to. Plan an activity following the test, regardless of the outcome, such as going to a movie or getting ice cream.

When you are taking the test, if you find yourself beginning to feel anxious, remind yourself that you know the material. Visualize successfully completing the test. Then take a few deep, relaxing breaths and return to it. Work through the questions carefully but with confidence, knowing that you are capable of succeeding.

Developing a healthy mental approach to test taking will also aid in other areas of life. Test anxiety affects more than just the actual test—it can be damaging to your mental health and even contribute to depression. It's important to beat test anxiety before it becomes a problem for more than testing.

Study Strategy

Being prepared for the test is necessary to combat anxiety, but what does being prepared look like? You may study for hours on end and still not feel prepared. What you need is a strategy for test prep. The next few pages outline our recommended steps to help you plan out and conquer the challenge of preparation.

Step 1: Scope Out the Test

Learn everything you can about the format (multiple choice, essay, etc.) and what will be on the test. Gather any study materials, course outlines, or sample exams that may be available. Not only will this help you to prepare, but knowing what to expect can help to alleviate test anxiety.

Step 2: Map Out the Material

Look through the textbook or study guide and make note of how many chapters or sections it has. Then divide these over the time you have. For example, if a book has 15 chapters and you have five days to study, you need to cover three chapters each day. Even better, if you have the time, leave an extra day at the end for overall review after you have gone through the material in depth.

If time is limited, you may need to prioritize the material. Look through it and make note of which sections you think you already have a good grasp on, and which need review. While you are studying, skim quickly through the familiar sections and take more time on the challenging parts.

Write out your plan so you don't get lost as you go. Having a written plan also helps you feel more in control of the study, so anxiety is less likely to arise from feeling overwhelmed at the amount to cover.

Step 3: Gather Your Tools

Decide what study method works best for you. Do you prefer to highlight in the book as you study and then go back over the highlighted portions? Or do you type out notes of the important information? Or is it helpful to make flashcards that you can carry with you? Assemble the pens, index cards, highlighters, post-it notes, and any other materials you may need so you won't be distracted by getting up to find things while you study.

If you're having a hard time retaining the information or organizing your notes, experiment with different methods. For example, try color-coding by subject with colored pens, highlighters, or post-it notes. If you learn better by hearing, try recording yourself reading your notes so you can listen while in the car, working out, or simply sitting at your desk. Ask a friend to quiz you from your flashcards, or try teaching someone the material to solidify it in your mind.

Step 4: Create Your Environment

It's important to avoid distractions while you study. This includes both the obvious distractions like visitors and the subtle distractions like an uncomfortable chair (or a too-comfortable couch that makes you want to fall asleep). Set up the best study environment possible: good lighting and a comfortable work area. If background music helps you focus, you may want to turn it on, but otherwise keep the room quiet. If you are using a computer to take notes, be sure you don't have any other windows open, especially applications like social media, games, or anything else that could distract you. Silence your phone and turn off notifications. Be sure to keep water close by so you stay hydrated while you study (but avoid unhealthy drinks and snacks).

Also, take into account the best time of day to study. Are you freshest first thing in the morning? Try to set aside some time then to work through the material. Is your mind clearer in the afternoon or evening? Schedule your study session then. Another method is to study at the same time of day that you will take the test, so that your brain gets used to working on the material at that time and will be ready to focus at test time.

Step 5: Study!

Once you have done all the study preparation, it's time to settle into the actual studying. Sit down, take a few moments to settle your mind so you can focus, and begin to follow your study plan. Don't give in to distractions or let yourself procrastinate. This is your time to prepare so you'll be ready to fearlessly approach the test. Make the most of the time and stay focused.

Of course, you don't want to burn out. If you study too long you may find that you're not retaining the information very well. Take regular study breaks. For example, taking five minutes out of every hour to walk briskly, breathing deeply and swinging your arms, can help your mind stay fresh.

As you get to the end of each chapter or section, it's a good idea to do a quick review. Remind yourself of what you learned and work on any difficult parts. When you feel that you've mastered the material, move on to the next part. At the end of your study session, briefly skim through your notes again.

But while review is helpful, cramming last minute is NOT. If at all possible, work ahead so that you won't need to fit all your study into the last day. Cramming overloads your brain with more information than it can process and retain, and your tired mind may struggle to recall even previously learned information when it is overwhelmed with last-minute study. Also, the urgent nature of cramming and the stress placed on your brain contribute to anxiety. You'll be more likely to go to the test feeling unprepared and having trouble thinking clearly.

So don't cram, and don't stay up late before the test, even just to review your notes at a leisurely pace. Your brain needs rest more than it needs to go over the information again. In fact, plan to finish your studies by noon or early afternoon the day before the test. Give your brain the rest of the day to relax or focus on other things, and get a good night's sleep. Then you will be fresh for the test and better able to recall what you've studied.

Step 6: Take a Practice Test

Many courses offer sample tests, either online or in the study materials. This is an excellent resource to check whether you have mastered the material, as well as to prepare for the test format and environment.

Check the test format ahead of time: the number of questions, the type (multiple choice, free response, etc.), and the time limit. Then create a plan for working through them. For example, if you have 30 minutes to take a 60-question test, your limit is 30 seconds per question. Spend less time on the questions you know well so that you can take more time on the difficult ones.

If you have time to take several practice tests, take the first one open book, with no time limit. Work through the questions at your own pace and make sure you fully understand them. Gradually work up to taking a test under test conditions: sit at a desk with all study materials put away and set a timer. Pace yourself to make sure you finish the test with time to spare and go back to check your answers if you have time.

After each test, check your answers. On the questions you missed, be sure you understand why you missed them. Did you misread the question (tests can use tricky wording)? Did you forget the information? Or was it something you hadn't learned? Go back and study any shaky areas that the practice tests reveal.

Taking these tests not only helps with your grade, but also aids in combating test anxiety. If you're already used to the test conditions, you're less likely to worry about it, and working through tests until you're scoring well gives you a confidence boost. Go through the practice tests until you feel comfortable, and then you can go into the test knowing that you're ready for it.

Test Tips

On test day, you should be confident, knowing that you've prepared well and are ready to answer the questions. But aside from preparation, there are several test day strategies you can employ to maximize your performance.

First, as stated before, get a good night's sleep the night before the test (and for several nights before that, if possible). Go into the test with a fresh, alert mind rather than staying up late to study.

Try not to change too much about your normal routine on the day of the test. It's important to eat a nutritious breakfast, but if you normally don't eat breakfast at all, consider eating just a protein bar. If you're a coffee drinker, go ahead and have your normal coffee. Just make sure you time it so that the caffeine doesn't wear off right in the middle of your test. Avoid sugary beverages, and drink enough water to stay hydrated but not so much that you need a restroom break 10 minutes into the test. If your test isn't first thing in the morning, consider going for a walk or doing a light workout before the test to get your blood flowing.

Allow yourself enough time to get ready, and leave for the test with plenty of time to spare so you won't have the anxiety of scrambling to arrive in time. Another reason to be early is to select a good seat. It's helpful to sit away from doors and windows, which can be distracting. Find a good seat, get out your supplies, and settle your mind before the test begins.

When the test begins, start by going over the instructions carefully, even if you already know what to expect. Make sure you avoid any careless mistakes by following the directions.

Then begin working through the questions, pacing yourself as you've practiced. If you're not sure on an answer, don't spend too much time on it, and don't let it shake your confidence. Either skip it and come back later, or eliminate as many wrong answers as possible and guess among the remaining ones. Don't dwell on these questions as you continue—put them out of your mind and focus on what lies ahead.

Be sure to read all of the answer choices, even if you're sure the first one is the right answer. Sometimes you'll find a better one if you keep reading. But don't second-guess yourself if you do immediately know the answer. Your gut instinct is usually right. Don't let test anxiety rob you of the information you know.

If you have time at the end of the test (and if the test format allows), go back and review your answers. Be cautious about changing any, since your first instinct tends to be correct, but make sure you didn't misread any of the questions or accidentally mark the wrong answer choice. Look over any you skipped and make an educated guess.

At the end, leave the test feeling confident. You've done your best, so don't waste time worrying about your performance or wishing you could change anything. Instead, celebrate the successful completion of this test. And finally, use this test to learn how to deal with anxiety even better next time.

Review Video: Test Anxiety
Visit mometrix.com/academy and enter code: 100340

Important Qualification

Not all anxiety is created equal. If your test anxiety is causing major issues in your life beyond the classroom or testing center, or if you are experiencing troubling physical symptoms related to your anxiety, it may be a sign of a serious physiological or psychological condition. If this sounds like your situation, we strongly encourage you to seek professional help.

Online Resources

Due to our efforts to try to keep this book to a manageable length, we've created a link that will give you access to all of your online resources:

mometrix.com/resources719/apmusictheory

It's Your Moment, Let's Celebrate It!

Share your story @mometrixtestpreparation